Colin Welland was born in Liverpool and began his career as an art teacher in a secondary modern school in Lancashire. Four years later he landed his first acting role, and eventually he was chosen for the part of Dave Graham in the popular TV series 'Z Cars'. Since then he has become a familiar face on television and in films, winning an award as Best Supporting Film Actor for *Kes*. In addition, he has written over 30 plays for television as well as the films *Yanks* and *Chariots of Fire*, winner of four Oscars including Best Film and Best Screenplay.

Colin is married to Pat, a former school teacher, and they live in London with their four children.

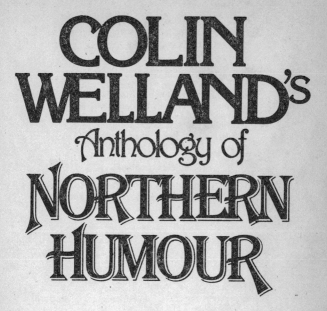

COLIN WELLAND's Anthology of NORTHERN HUMOUR

Cartoons by 'Albert'

Hamlyn Paperbacks

COLIN WELLAND'S
ANTHOLOGY OF NORTHERN HUMOUR
ISBN 0600 20202 X

First published in Great Britain 1982
by Hamlyn Paperbacks
Copyright © Introduction, compilation and
original material 1982 by Colin Welland

Hamlyn Paperbacks are published by
The Hamlyn Publishing Group Ltd,
Astronaut House,
Feltham,
Middlesex, England

Reproduced, printed and bound in Great Britain by
Hazell Watson & Viney Ltd, Aylesbury, Bucks

CONTENTS

Acknowledgements

The author and publisher wish to thank the following for permission to quote material written or published by them in this book: Mr Eddie Braben for extracts from scripts written by him for Eric Morecambe and Ernie Wise; Dalesman Books, for permission to quote from *Lancashire Nicknames and Sayings* by Bob Dobson (1973); Mrs H. L. Gee for extracts from *Yorkshire Wit and Humour* by H. L. Gee (1962) Victor Gollancz, London for extracts from *Goodbye to Yorkshire* by Roy Hattersley (1976); Macdonald Futura Publishers, London, for extracts from *The Thoughts of Trueman Now* by Fred Trueman, Eric Morecambe and William Rushton (1979); Frederick Muller, London, for extracts from *Sing As We Go* by Gracie Fields (1960); the *Observer* newspaper for extracts from 'The Survival of the Little Waster' by Richard Kelly, published in the *Observer Magazine*, 1979; Souvenir Press, London, for extracts from *Cardus in the Covers* by Neville Cardus (1978); Times Newspapers Limited for extracts from two articles, 'Where the Elite Meet to Eat' by Gordon Burn and 'Funny Girl' by David Robson, published in the *Sunday Times Magazine*, (1980); and Woburn Press, London, for extracts from *Before Your Very Eyes* by Arthur Askey (1975).

Introduction

I've lived amongst Londoners for twenty-odd years and I still think that, on the whole, they're a pretty humourless lot. Perhaps it's the part of London I live in; perhaps if I chatted through life amongst East Enders or down Clapham or Tooting I might revise my opinion as I believe they've a chirpy resilience all of their own. In fact, I *know* they have, having been on the end of a sharp Cockney crack more times than I've drunk flat pints – and down South that's a *lot*. But I live in posh, middle-class SW13, and life down that way is pretty unfunny, what with immense mortgage payments to find, school fees, two cars to run . . . poor souls.

So when I go back up North amongst the wage-packet millions, who for generations have never had a worry save one – where the next penny's coming from; and never more so than today – I cannot help but wonder at the almost compulsory laughter and self-deprecating banter which washes into every nook and cranny of their lives.

Why *are* Northerners so ready to laugh? Why *is* humour such an integral and indispensable part of their concept of what day-to-day living is about? Get on a bus in the early, early hours in Leeds or Wigan, the windows filthy, the air stiff with fog and frost, the top deck a mobile cancer ward of cigarette smoke and bronchial coughs; the conductor will clatter upstairs in a rattle of change and cry, 'Any more fares on the sunshine roof?' If he tried it on the Number 9 to Hammersmith he'd risk prosecution for disturbing the misery.

Northern humour to Southern ears is coarse, dangerously near insulting, more often than not in bad taste, yet compelling, fascinating and irresistible. Standing in a Berkshire pub, all beams, brass and Bass, after a cricket match the other day, I happened to mention that I thought manners were improving round Wigan way, that fellows I had known back home as rather rustic brutes were nowadays ironing out the creases and occasionally behaving like human beings – men like Bill

7

Duckworth, a particularly animal-like prop forward I used to play rugby with. Retired from the game now, he spends his Saturdays reffing the odd junior game. A couple of weeks ago he surprised us all by, at the sight of a passing funeral cortège, stopping the game and demanding that the players bow their heads in respect. Afterwards, I complimented him on the dignity of his action. 'It was the least I could do,' he replied. 'We were married twenty-five years.' The club, too, was deeply impressed. Instead of merely realizing enough for a wreath, the collection had totalled several hundred pounds. Bill, moved and grateful, decided to buy a headstone for his wife's grave. The monumental mason was very helpful in suggesting a lovely piece of Welsh slate. Bill spelt out the simple dedication: 'Elsie Duckworth, died Jan 20th 1979. Sorely missed by husband William. "She was thine."' 'Leave it all to me,' said the mason. 'I'll put one of my best lads on it. I'll give you a ring when it's ready and in position and you can nip up to the cemetery and have a look.'

Within a couple of days Bill was climbing up through the graves to view his newly acquired piece of Welsh slate. It looked lovely, polished and glistening, the lettering clear-cut and crisp: 'Elsie Duckworth. Died Jan 20th 1979. Sorely missed by husband William. "She was thin."'

Quite naturally Bill was a bit upset. He confronted the mason with his complaint: 'He's left the "e" out.' 'I don't believe it,' replied the man. 'Just shows, if you want a job done properly, do it yourself. Leave it to me. Have a look in the morning and you won't know the difference.'

The following morning, Bill was there, cap in hand, re-reading his precious slate: 'Elsie Duckworth. Died Jan 20th 1979. Sorely missed by husband William. "Ee, she was thin."'

Funerals, deaths, tragedies, all are fair game for a Northern gag. Strict taboos in the tight-arsed South are perfectly natural hunting grounds for the North's rampaging comedians.

A fellow I knew came back after five years abroad. He

decided to look up an old pal, but his wife answered the door weeping: 'George has passed away,' she sobbed. 'We'd been to Blackpool for us holidays and when we came back a-Sunday I sent him down to the allotment to pick us a cabbage for dinner. He bent down and keeled over just like that – dead as mutton.' My mate was shocked. 'Good God, love, I *am* sorry,' he said. 'What did you do?' 'Well,' she replied, composing herself, 'we had to open a tin of peas.'

Naturally very upset, my friend asked if he might go in and view the body – pay his respects. 'Yes,' said the wife, 'but shut the door after you, the cats have had him on the roof three times.'

Led into the front room, he gazed down at the corpse of his old friend lying serene in its coffin. 'Ee!' he said, 'he does look well.' 'I should think he does,' said the wife, 'he's just had a week in Blackpool.'

The Co-op are always very tasteful and they supply the boiled ham sandwiches.

Co-op

TESCO

Bred in deeply depressed times when life was so bitterly hard that the only sanctuary was laughter, Northern wit, in the soft underbelly of England, is unnerving. They laugh fit to bust but, as they do, glance around and over shoulders, seeking their group's approval, reassuring themselves that their instincts are right and it really is funny.

In the pages to follow are conversations with many Northerners from all walks of life, every one of them successful and celebrated. To some, humour is a profession; the others are all enthusiastic amateurs. All are happiest when enjoying the broad, flat, uncompromisingly vulgar rhetoric of the classic Northern tale.

An old pal of mine took his wife out for a meal last weekend. 'Lovely it was,' he said, 'tandoori, you know. T'wife could live on it. . . . But when we got home, we'd been broken into – burgled. What a bloody mess – plates smashed, furniture all over, sheets ripped, cushions busted open, filthy writing on t'wall. . . . And, d'you know, we'd a tin of hot pot on t'stove, and t'buggers'd crapped in it.' He sighed and shook his head: 'We had to throw half of it away!'

Northern humour – I love it, d'you see? To sit in a Northern working-class pub with a pint of milky-headed bitter and the banter all about, whilst not *exactly* my idea of heaven, is pretty close to it. I'd settle for a heaven that's as vital, honest and which attacks life or death, as the case may be, with such vigour and complete lack of pretension. Conversation is still of paramount import in Northern social life. If you can't verbally give and take, you're dead. Even the bloke standing like a statue behind his ale apparently impervious to all around him is far from it. He's odds-on to provide the final *coup de grâce* in any violent discussion around him. And there's nowhere sacred either: funeral parlours, church, dentists, doctors – all come under the caustic whip some time or other, and none more than the sports arena.

I remember watching an amateur Rugby League match one Sunday morning. It was like bloody Hades up there on a gale-swept slag heap – the two pub teams beating hell out of each other on a pitch of shit and cinders. After a particularly violent piece of argument, in front of us, play trundled away, leaving one poor lad heaving himself to his feet in an armour of mud-sodden kit, his face spattered with blood, the gale beating rain into his bloodshot eyes. He dragged his sleeve across his mouth and sighed. 'By the bloody hell,' he grunted, 'I'll be glad when it's cricket season!'

Northerners, too, have an implicit, brave and sometimes touching faith in the belief that a good wisecrack conquers all. An instance of this that springs to mind occurred when I was on tour with my local rugby team – Union this time: it makes little difference round our neck of the woods – and we were on the Isle of Man, which is renowned for its exquisite draught Bass. Mainly out of idle curiosity, the lads had decided to partake of a sample and the following morning our hotel was virtually uninhabitable. An elephant's graveyard would have smelt sweeter. As it was quite an expensive hotel, the more sensitive of us felt more than a little remorse as we crept down for breakfast. Not so our little scrum half – a pit man – who was known for his almost suicidal confidence in his own wit. He stepped into the dining room full of truculent fellow guests and called for silence. The shocked assembly paused between bacon and egg and looked at him.

'Ladies and gentlemen,' he announced, 'I realize that us lads were on draught Bass last night and that the atmosphere in the hotel leaves a lot to be desired . . . but I do object when the chamber maid comes in, to make my bed, with a canary.'

It's hard, isn't it, to resist? Part of the charm is the Northerner's ability to laugh at himself. The same rugby mob came down to London once to watch one of the internationals at Twickenham. I joined the coach at Richmond and the lads were already far down the well-trodden way to oblivion. The game was to be against France, and a coach full of partisans drew up alongside us. This brought out all that was best and British in my comrades: 'Wogs!' they chanted into the bemused Gallic faces alongside us, 'wogs! wogs! wogs!' An old contemporary of mine, seated alongside me, sighed and said, 'Colin, we were in an 'Ungarian restaurant last night . . . and after that I'm in no doubt as to who are the wogs!'

People often call me a professional Northerner and they intend to be disparaging, but I take it as a compliment. Anyone who can make a good living simply by being what they are must be on a good wicket. And it says a lot, too, for the entertainment value of the culture from which they sprang.

The North of England must be one of the few places in the world where humour has been honed so fine as to be found in the miserable. Two old miners were stood at the bar of their palatial working-man's club watching the cabaret. A lamé-suited American comedian was rattling out his act perched on a high stool, brittle, sharp and scintillating. One old pit man turned to the other and asked, 'What d'you think of the comic?' The other thought for a minute, pulled on his pint and answered, 'He's all right . . . if you like laughing!'

Well, I *do* like laughing – it makes life worth living. I was failed for a commission in the army. The reason given? 'An over-developed sense of humour.' Well, I didn't get a pip but, by God, I've enjoyed myself since.

I hope you enjoy what my fellow Northerners have to say . . . they've always got a chuckle just round the corner of their mouths, like me. Perhaps it's a thankless task trying to define Northern humour – it's like what the Irish poet said about critics: 'They'd cut a skylark's throat to see what makes it sing.' But maybe in trying, dwelling on its substance for a while, we'll reveal its qualities to those who hitherto haven't caught the bug. I hope so.

Colin Welland

The Professionals

I was born in Liverpool, and in the dark early days of the war, we kids used to sit in front of the fire clutching our meagre sweet rations, switch on the wireless and laugh with 'Bandwagon' and 'ITMA'. Yet Arthur Askey and Tommy Handley were only two of the multitude of comics whose Northern patter carried a nation through the worst crisis in its history. We also had Frank Randle, Albert Modley, George Formby, Sandy Powell, Dave Morris and Norman Evans, with their world of landladies and despotic bosses, doctors, Blackpool and fish and chips, rent-men, policemen, toffs to be punctured . . . and bourgeois pretentiousness to be shot down in flames. It was a landscape of working-class double-dealing and pain to be borne with a patient self-ridicule; a world of dentures and garden walls to be talked over, cats in the custard and drawers on the line, boobs and bowels and bottoms, hounded husbands and back-handing wives. For every Max Miller and Tommy Trinder there were dozens of Scousers, Lankies and Yorkies aching to be laughed with, and at, at the end of every pier or in every concert party, in or out of uniform. Ask any ex-serviceman where the comics come from in their outfit. Why *were* there so many? Why *are* there so many? Think of your favourites today: Eric and Ernie, Ken Dodd, Jimmy Tarbuck, Les Dawson, Duggie Brown – you can go on for ever. What is it about the land north of Stoke which produces such a harvest of funnymen? If you ask the funnymen themselves, they will all point in one direction, to the fountain head, the source for the beginning of an answer: I mean, of course, the incomparable Jimmy James.

Jimmy James

I never saw Jimmy 'live', but remember wetting myself with regular monotony at his tatty, top-hatted drunk on the TV. With his broken cigarette and weaving between two stooges, he perfected an approach to comedy which pointed the way for many of the famous still to come. Sid Fields, Tony Hancock

13

would have admitted and Frankie Howerd will admit their debt to the little genius. A teetotaller himself, James managed, with a staggering attention to detail, to pinpoint the essential psychology of a rolling drunk, his desperate desire to prove himself sober. He also had that inborn Northern talent of being able to say things funnily, rather than to say funny things. He didn't beg a laugh with a punch line – he didn't believe in them; he merely asked us to watch ourselves and our surrounding world, recognize its utter ridiculousness – and laugh at it. And his world was of the Northern working class . . . and how they loved him.

I talked to James's son, Jimmy Casey, now light-entertainment producer at the BBC, Manchester, about his father. One picture he conjured up seems to epitomize the secret of James's common touch. He remembers acting out new routines with his dad before his mother's critical eye as she sat up in a big brass bed in their digs. If she laughed, the new routine went into the act. So much for some of the synthetic middle-of-the-road, plastic, 'semi-detached' comedy of today – it would not survive such an exacting test. Here's what else Jimmy's son said:

Jimmy James started trends which other comics followed. You can see the debt people like Tony Hancock and Morecambe and Wise owe to my father in their work. On the other hand, the two things which every comic in the business admires about Jimmy –his sense of timing and his ad-libbing – very few can equal.

Even the Goons were like Jimmy in certain areas of their comedy; the surrealism, combined with the down-to-earth quality in their work, was very much a part of Jimmy James as well. His act with the two stooges could become very surrealistic and lunatic, a lot of it ad-libbed, too.

Spike Milligan of the Goons wrote a song, 'I'm Walking Backwards for Christmas', which was not unlike one of Jimmy's in style:

JJ: She was sitting at the seaside getting brown, brown, brown,
And the sea was coming up, up, up.

> She had no one to guide her as she gathered shells and
>   whelks,
> So she fell in love with the first boy scout she saw; It
>   was reveal . . .

Stooge: Shouldn't it be reveille?

JJ: Yes, but it doesn't rhyme.

Jimmy James was among the first to use a stooge – or two – in his act. Hylda Baker used one, of course, and Tony Hancock and Frankie Howerd both used a stage pianist. Even Vic Oliver, who had always been a solo performer, suddenly started having a stooge around for a while. Where my father was different was in his attitude to his stooges. Although they were two obvious idiots, he still believed in them. He would say, or would announce to the audience, 'He is going to do this' or 'He is going to sing', and would believe it himself. If the stooge told him he had a lion in the box under his arm, Jimmy would say, 'Yes, I thought I heard a rustling.'

'There'll be room in the van for the three of us,' he would say.

Mind you, he never analyzed this attitude in his life. It just happened, just grew out of his own warm personality.

Jimmy had two basic acts, the drunk ('toper' was *not* a word of his), and the act with the stooges. The drunk act varied very little, but the stooges act varied with different themes over the years. They might put in a line and within a week be doing as much as four minutes on it, having dropped four minutes of something else.

We were playing at the Newcastle Empire once, our main theme being the chipsters routine. (This was about the art of making potato chips.) I remarked that perhaps we ought to drop it – meaning some time in the future – because most people had seen it a couple of times, and maybe we should stop using it while it was still very big and work on another routine to replace it. This was Tuesday morning. Jimmy said, 'Right, we'll cut it out tonight.' There was an enormous row, of course, because you couldn't just cut out ten minutes which had taken weeks, even months, of work to get together. It's different today, when there is a lot of padding in most acts, but those days in variety

15

you were given a strictly limited time. If you were given eighteen minutes, you didn't do twenty. Everything was a honed and definitive performance. To remove ten minutes out of that chipster act for that night was apparently impossible. Anyway, he did, and by the end of the week had produced an entire new routine to do with Indian music and the stooge's being a half-caste. It was fantastically successful.

The main thing about Jimmy was his tremendous confidence. It's one reason why he was such a good ad-libber. He was a *true* ad-libber, unlike Ted Ray and the like, who would have hundreds of things ready to 'ad-lib' with. Jimmy James ad-libbed totally – he had an incredibly quick mind. He *never* told a joke – he hated telling jokes – and he never ad-libbed with some smart wisecrack. His ad-libs usually tended to be subtle remarks or fantastic stories, like the one he told when he was doing a television show in Manchester when television was just starting there. The production assistant on the show was pretty ignorant, and he had not done his homework either: 'Now, Mr James, what exactly do you do?' Jimmy looked at him, and went off into this fantastic thing. 'I'm glad you asked that, because he's [turning to his stooge of that time] been worrying about it. We do an act dressed as Chinese on trapezes, spinning bowls of goldfish on a string from our teeth. It's the centrifugal force, you see. When the bowls spin out wide, will there be enough room in here? He's worried about it, you see!' By this time, the PA was worried too, and went off to find out!

Jimmy would force his stooges to ad-lib too. If you didn't come back with something, and something that was good so that he could get laughs from it, he'd say, 'What's the matter with you? Your bloody cue's stuck!' Then you'd start doing things on stage and try to catch him, but you never did. This is what comedians loved about him: other comedians don't work like that. Their attitude is: 'I'll change things, you do the lines.' Every comedian who ever worked with Jimmy James watched his act twice every night.

I remember a time when Eli Woods very nearly did catch him out – but not quite. They were working together, and Eli came out with a tremendous laugh. He is a very funny man, and when he delivers a funny line, it *is* a funny line. To top him is not easy. Anyway, they were doing the routine of the stooge with a cardboard box or shoe box. In it he had a real lion, a real giraffe and, finally, an elephant.

JJ: Is it a male or a female?

Eli: No, it's an elephant.

JJ: It must be a male or a female. But I don't suppose it would make any difference to you.

Eli: I d-d-don't suppose it would make any difference to anyone except another elephant.

JJ: I'll have to stop you going to these youth clubs.

The line was delivered with extreme seriousness, and was a great ad-lib.

Off-stage, too, ad-libbing and creating fantastic pictures were second nature to Jimmy. There is a lovely story of his going backstage after one of Ken Dodd's performances at Blackpool. There was a girl singer, whom Jimmy congratulated on her lovely act.

'Thanks,' she said. 'Are you in the business?'

'No, no. I'm what you theatricals call stage-struck. I'm a plumber. I have twelve businesses, built out of nothing. Have you got a minute?'

'Yes.'

So he went on for about twelve minutes, about how he invented the underwipe, in six months had three shops, in two years a couple of dozen. . . . 'Now I'm retired. Just collect the money.'

It was all told with complete conviction. She stayed to listen, though bored stiff, because he said he had liked her act.

There was another time when this tremendous confidence, plus the ability to ad-lib, worked wonders. He was working at the Palladium and only doing one act. I was not in this act, but I was writing for it. There was an argument on the Sunday before about which act he would do. In the end, Jimmy said he would not do any of the ones discussed: he would do the Festival of Britain act. Now this act, which we had written for a radio broadcast, only ran to eight minutes, and Jimmy was supposed to be doing eighteen minutes on the Palladium. Jimmy said, 'We'll pad it out,' and once again there was a big argument – you know, I never argued with any other performers I worked with, only my father – and we all said he was insane. But nothing would stop him, so, unbelievably, he *tried out a new act at the Palladium*! No one else would have done it.

The stooge at the time was Dick Carlton, and he was petrified. He walked on and, instead of saying, 'Welcome to the Festival of Britain,' said 'Welcome to the Battle of Britain.' Then he froze. Jimmy James ran on and explained why to the audience. 'It's Monday night and the lad's nervous. And all you lot with your free tickets . . .' Eli Woods, the other stooge, was brought into this with some ad-libbing about a barrow of fruit and 'Harvest Festival'. There was about fifteen minutes of this, then the poor stooge was sent off. He came on again, managed to announce, 'Welcome to the Festival of Britain' – and got a standing ovation.

Telling the truth like that to the audience is something Eric Morecambe does. He always makes a big point of saying Ernie has gone wrong.

Jimmy's ad-libbing used to stand him in good stead when things went wrong, too. I remember a time when there was a problem with the scenery and my father went on while we fixed it. He ad-libbed for about seven minutes, and got a tremendous reaction. All I can remember about it was that it had been snowing for two weeks, so there had been no football, and he went on as a drunk, saying how sorry he felt for Mr Vernon and Mr Littlewood. During the interval he was going to go into the auditorium and raffle a duck for them. When he came off he said, 'What did I say? There were some good lines there and I can't remember them.'

Then there was a time during the blitz in the Midlands, when we were doing two Sunday concerts. I was with him on holiday from school with my cousin, Jack Casey (who now uses the stage name Eli Woods). One stooge couldn't make it to the theatre because no taxi driver would take him through the bombing. He finally arrived in time for the second concert, so we did one and a quarter hours on our own. My father made a speech, all of it ad-libbed from the top of his head, about the courage of Britain, with the sound of a machine-gun and bombs falling in the distance. A land-mine blew in the back door of the theatre and Jimmy shouted, 'Make up your mind – are you coming in or not? It's a wedding party!' At the same time, he was also apparently talking to a terrified politician in the wings. He finished by saying, 'I will sing "Begin the Beguine" . . . [then was totally drowned in the sound of machine-gun fire] . . . with drum accompaniment.' Cheers from the audience.

As for Jimmy James's sense of timing – well, he used to say the greatest timer was Robb Wilton, and Robb used to say, 'There's only one timer and that's your father.' They had a mutual admiration society going. The thing about timing is that you can see its effect when a comedian gets a very big laugh with a look or a not-very-funny line. Jack Benny and George Burns are superb, and Eric Morecambe is one of the best timers today. The essence of it is having repose, confidence and the courage to wait until everybody's interest is centred on you. *Then* you say it; *then* you do it. The greatest lesson I learned from watching my father is that a sense of timing can't be taught.

It was very significant to his success that Jimmy James was born in the North. The Northern language is wonderful material to use in comedy. A Southern comedian who normally speaks in an ordinary Southern voice will adopt a special voice to be funny, perhaps broad Cockney, or a 'Cyril Fletcher' voice. Even Stanley Holloway adopted a Northern voice for his monologues. The Northern accent lends itself to comedy because it makes words sound funny and there is a warmth as well. Speed comes into it, too. The Northern comic tends to have more repose. The Southern comic tends to tell you how clever he is and how he comes out on top, whereas the Northern one tends to tell you how someone made a fool of him. He reaches out for sympathy and warmth.

Liverpool humour, for example, is fantastic, with a firm edge to the talk and a lot of wit and warmth. Everyone in Liverpool is a comedian. I was on a bus there early in the morning once, and the conductor said to a woman passenger, 'Don't go upstairs, luv, I haven't made the beds yet.'

Another time, two old ladies were getting on an empty bus and the conductor shouted, 'Room for two standing only!'

Or there was the one who started off: 'Good morning, everyone, this is your conductor speaking. We shall be travelling at a speed of 36 miles an hour . . .'

The choice of the right word was very important in Jimmy's work, where getting a single word right would be absolutely essential. Mind you, most of it was instinct, especially on stage, where we had no script. Everything started with a basic theme, then developed on stage. Jimmy did do radio and TV, but he preferred the stage. It was his to dominate. He never really had a series that took off on radio, and he was never successful on television, largely because in his day people were tied down too much by the script and fitting it into a set time. Ken Dodd's the same: the best he has done on television is half what he achieves on stage, where he is devastating.

Jimmy James was uncomfortable doing television. One *dire* series called 'Meet the Champ' was a mistake. I'd done an act as a boxing trainer with Eli as the potential champ. Then the idea came up of doing a series, but using Bernard Breslaw, not Eli. The whole thing was wrongly written and Jimmy was tied down in what he was doing and saying. The only time the series had life was when he put many of his own lines into it and got Eli into it. Jimmy had to have freedom to move in order to say what he wanted to say.

He used to do some terrible things on radio, too, and we would have terrible rows. Once we were broadcasting in Blackpool. I had written a script for him, Eli and me. My father walked on and dropped his script. He refused to read mine and instead started telling the listeners what had happened. 'It's not right. My script had no paper clip. Surely the BBC can afford three paper clips.' In a nine-minute broadcast we did not do a single line of the script. Eli stood around for about four minutes and did not speak a line. Jimmy turned to him and Eli said, 'I haven't had a word to say.' JJ replied, 'No, but you have been thinking, I can tell.' Came the reply, 'I was thinking, this is a hell of a place to rehearse.' 'All right,' said JJ, 'I'll look at your script. What's the last line?' I said the last line, and of course no one knew what we were talking about. They played the music and that was it.

Jimmy also lost his script in a Hancock programme. They did not do a single line of the sketch about railways which Galton and Simpson had written. Instead, Jimmy talked to Tony Hancock about a fellow walking about London without a bag of salt in his crisps: someone must have had two bags, and his chips would be too salty. Tony was white-faced with terror because he was not an ad-libber. Mind you, he was a great Jimmy James fan thereafter, as was Frankie Howerd. Once Frankie put a line into a script which killed Jimmy's next line, so that there was no point in saying it. 'That line's not in the script, you know,' he said, turning to Frankie. 'Why didn't you tell me you were going to do that?' – and he threw his script into the audience. There were five more minutes without a script.

It was this unpredictability of my father's that made other

performers rather scared of him; it was also another reason why television did not work very well for him. He could reduce other actors to helpless laughter, too, while remaining unsmiling himself – he never smiled. There was a 'Sunday Night at the Prince of Wales' with Billy Dainty, where my father had to do a little bit at the beginning which was unscripted. Billy would come on and say, 'Dainty. You're Jimmy James? I'm Dainty,' and my father would say, 'Well, that's your problem.' And every time Billy could not go on for laughing. There was also the occasion when Jimmy was rehearsing with Harry Secombe and had Harry literally on the floor with laughter. My father just kept apologizing very seriously to the producer, and the more he apologized, the more Harry laughed.

In fact, my father took his work very seriously. The *reality* of the performance was essential to him. For instance, if the script called for a line to be whispered in his ear, it had to be the right line, not a mumble, even though Jimmy knew what the line should be and even though the audience could not hear. For example, we used to do a joke about a pianist trying to find a note and getting all round it but not on it. 'Let's try on a violin – that piano's damp,' he would say. Then: 'That's an old violin.' 'It's an old master,' one of us would reply. There would be a bit of double talk, and he would say, 'Oh, a fiddle!' Then I would whisper in his ear and he would reply, 'Oh, I did, too – it's an old master!' The first time I did this, I just mumbled in his ear and didn't bother to speak the line properly. Afterwards Jimmy said, 'You *must* say it. You're supposed to say, "I thought he said 'bastard'," so *say* it. How am I supposed to know what he said?' This was why every performance was new to him: you listen to what the other fellow is saying and then react to it. So nothing goes stale.

It was this sense of the importance of reality and a belief in what he was doing that made Jimmy James's work so unforgettable, unique. He was always reckoned to be the great drunk, for instance, even though he was a teetotaller in private life. He used to say, 'Your *ankles* have got to be drunk. A drunk is limp. He falls down and doesn't hurt himself.'

For the same reason, his visual gags with cigarettes were

always successful. He would do them casually, apparently without thinking, as though they were natural to him. He would stamp out a cigarette while he was talking, lift his foot, take the butt from the sole of his shoe and transfer it to his pocket, all absolutely unconscious of his own actions. The implication was that he always did it because he saved the butts.

Then there was the cigarette gag used in his drunk sketch when he was rowing with his wife. She would walk out of the room; he, in his stockinged feet, would throw down his cigarette while shouting into the next room, and stand on the cigarette. He would never react until he felt the cigarette burning. By the end of the week he would have burnt through a pair of socks.

Things *must* be real, then the reaction is real. Probably that is why Jimmy James is still remembered among actors today. He died in 1964, but many people who worked with him still stop me and tell me lovingly remembered stories about him. They've all got their own personal story of something he said or did.

Les Dawson

Les Dawson remains for me one of the last great funnymen of the old tradition. At his best when faced with a live audience, he recaptures for me all the earthy, mock-evil, scandal-mongering rumbustiousness of Northern day-to-day banter. But he adds to it a degree of literacy which is often as unnerving as it is a delight. Sometimes I feel uncomfortable, asking whether he is too ambitious when he wanders off into one of his surrealistic tales, but Les never underestimates his audience and inevitably proves me wrong. We always fall about laughing, we're not as thick as we sometimes make out, and Les knows it. He told us something about his approach while seated in his dressing room at the Birmingham Hippodrome, where he was working in panto.

It was a mid-week matinée of *Babes in the Wood* and front of house was a great, shoving, giggling, sweetie-chewing mass of kids – about two thousand of them – plus mums and dads and a fair sprinkling of senior citizens. It was obviously going to be a full house.

Backstage, the tannoy had not begun broadcasting alerts to the company to take their places, and the orchestra was not yet tuning up in the pit. All was hushed and quiet. There was a smell of greasepaint, though, and movement from behind closed dressing-room doors as actors climbed into costume.

The door of Number 1 dressing room was open, and we were welcomed in by the star of the show. He's not exactly Robert Redford, is Les, undeniably fat, standing there in his gent's Y-fronts, over which he pulled the first item of his panto-dame outfit, an enormous pair of ladies' pink knee-length lock-knit bloomers. But he is much more approachable than the great Hollywood star; ready to talk at length about his life and work, to ensure that you get a good interview. He even found time just to sit and reminisce between his on-stage appearances and his several changes from one 'feminine' costume to another. Les remembers vividly his own working-class childhood in the Manchester of the 1930s, and sees the desperate unemployment of those days as the major influence on Northern humour.

'A lot of the jokes I grew up with were born of desperation – laugh rather than cry. All the traditional heavy industries of the North were sensitive to economic difficulties, whereas in the South, where they had a much greater diversification of light industry, there wasn't the same unemployment, even in the bad days, so their humour tended – and still does tend – to be on the surface. There wasn't as much depth to it as Northern humour. For the North, it was basically a struggle for survival. I mean, if cotton went down the pan then so did the whole of Lancashire, and the same with ship-building and Tyneside. Laugh or go under, it was then, and it is still very much the same. There's more depth, more acidity, more bite in Northern humour than there is in Southern. Nor are there the character comedians in the South that the North produces – the Frank Randles and Albert Modleys and all those people.'

Les agrees that the poverty and the desperation is not the same today as it was, but it is still remembered, and there is a romantic nostalgia about it all, so that he can still base what he is doing on it: 'Oh, yes, even today, you still can; it will be recognized, and the younger ones will say to you, "I remember me dad sayin' that, you know." That, I think, is the key to it.'

Les had no firm ambition to become a comic as he grew up. Somehow he found himself working the music halls at the tail end of their life, when the family audiences which had kept them going were being killed off by the halls' decay into nude reviews, and the comic entertainer was becoming little more than a compère for bilge with titles like 'Bareway to Stardom' and 'She Stoops to Conquer'. Then the clubs began to appear in the North: 'The big ones, two-thousand-seater sports halls, where one night they had wrestling, perhaps, and another night boxing or cabaret – but always with beer and scampi. They had a vitality about them. They were rough and ready, but they had something. They lost it when they got more sophisticated. They had to because there was television and people were going abroad and experienced the Continental night life. Even the most mundane of clubs has now become highly sophisticated, with expensive equipment, lighting and what-have-you. But you can still get away with budgie jokes and the like because, basically, humour never changes really.'

Robb Wilton and Frank Randle were two pre-war comics who influenced Les a lot. 'Robb's humour bridges the generations. He did that lovely gag about the day war broke out. The wife says to him, "What are you doing for the war effort?" And he says, "The Germans are occupying Dieppe, and there are six Panzer divisions going to land at Hastings and invade, so there are me and Harry Halfbottle and Big Harry, so we are all going down, the three of us, to form an ambush." She says, "There's only three of you?" and he answers, "You are forgetting the element of surprise."

'That's still the sort of thing you use today: the basic humour never changes. Everybody, at some time in their life, is going to be skint for a bob or two, and we can all experience economic hardship, whether in the thirties, forties or eighties – it makes no difference – so it'll always be there. Because it's human.'

'It's the same with mother-in-law jokes. There will always be mother-in-law jokes. The earliest recorded is a Roman joke – the one where the Roman tribune says to a soldier, "You volunteered to come from Syria to Britain. Why?" And the Roman soldier says, "To see my mother-in-law." "But your mother-in-law lives in Rome," says the tribune. Comes the reply: "She looks better from Britain." Mother-in-law jokes still go down well, and always will as long as man tries to make his mark against the encroachment of woman. Every woman is a matriarch at heart, so the mother-in-law is a perfect centre-piece.'

One of Les's own mother-in-law jokes is as follows: 'There was a knock on the front door and I knew it was my mother-in-law because the flowers on the sideboard wilted, and they're plastic. I opened the door and said, "Well, don't stand there in the pouring rain. Go home!"'

Then there's the version he threw off in a radio 'Woman's Hour' interview: 'The last seven years we've had the mother-in-law come for Christmas dinner. This year things will be different – we're going to let her in.'

When he goes in front of an audience, Les has a skeleton script in mind and a whole career of stories and jokes behind him to draw on. 'You have what you call standards which you know will get a laugh no matter how many times you tell them. It does not matter how old the joke is – it's how it's told, and there is always a generation growing up that hasn't heard it, so in a sense it's timeless. All that humour really does is mirror birth, life, sex, and the rent collector. The jokes are a foundation on which you can base your plot.

'I don't use jokes as such anyway. Just preamble, talk. I do a property routine which is basically very Northern, and it always goes down very well. It's terribly exaggerated, but there's a *kernel* of truth in it.'

Here Les settles himself comfortable in his chair, ignoring the squawks of the tannoy calling various actors into the wings, and goes into his property routine.

'I came from a poor family but we were happy on the whole – we lived in a hole. Give you an idea of how bad things were: we were trying to keep up with the Joneses next door and they were in the care of Oxfam. At the age of fifteen, I thought knives and forks were jewellery. All the clothes we wore were cast-offs, hand-me-downs. I started work at fifteen in bib and jumper suit and a bowler hat. And me sister – she got married in bush hat, trousers and spats . . .'

'That's the sort of thing – a long preamble of how bad things were. And then I go off into flights of fancy, with long monologues about rolling meadows and dreaming trees and hedgerows – and then I'll flatten it. That's the basic act which, by some miraculous power, seems to go down well.'

Les does not have to tailor any of this much for a theatre or club down South. 'You slow your delivery down, because the Southerner hasn't got the same quickness. That's the only difference.

'I never tell blue jokes or ethnic jokes. They are not going to solve anything, and anyway I don't think they are funny. I must have heard every bloody Irish joke there is now.

'My TV stuff is scripted much more tightly because of timing, and I have to keep off topical jokes. They are not all that marvellous anyway because a lot of people don't read the newspapers, or they may see something on TV but don't assimilate it anyway. Unless it is something patently obvious, I keep well off it. It's not worth it.'

After his Manchester upbringing, Les lived in London for many years, then he came back to the North. 'The quality of life's better here. I used to love London, but it's so over-expensive now, so much is a rip-off. They'll always produce more comics in the North than in the South, anyway. As someone once bitterly put it: "A lot of comics come from Liverpool – they've got to be a comic to live there." You know – that syndrome.'

At one time in his career, Les was a courier, escorting tours for a travel firm. He took parties to Europe, mostly in coaches, and to Spain. He can get by in several European languages, though he speaks Spanish best. 'One tour, I remember a meal in which we were having a magnificent dish – salmon cooked in champagne and, believe me, that's something. And there was a bloke from Doncaster. "That bloody food's rubbish," he said. "Why don't they do something like hamburger and chips?"'

He has written two novels, and is negotiating a film deal on one of them. Home is in Lytham St Annes, with its golf course (the golf clubs are propped up in a corner of the dressing room), old Victorian ladies, and a faded image it steadfastly refuses to lose, which is why he likes it, though he is not sure what the old Victorian ladies would make of his line of business.

'Fancy dressing like this every day. Something vaguely immoral about it, isn't there?' He's putting on nurse's uniform, plus the pink bloomers, a huge bra, knee-high stockings, ankle boots and curly wig. 'What I wear is always unashamedly butch, Norman Evans-style, with no pretensions to glamour. I'm not going to do a Danny la Rue. It makes them laugh and that's the name of the game. This panto we are doing has been going on for four months now and we change little bits every night. Just throw lines in, and they pick them up.'

One of his fellow actors is Eli Woods, tall, skinny and gangling, with a long, lugubrious and gentle face. Eli once worked with Jimmy James, and his experience is considerable. He's well able to pick up new lines thrown at him in the middle of a scene. Some lines don't change, however: 'When Eli says, "I'm not taking my clothes off," and I say, "If you did, you'd look like a dip-stick," the kids like it, so we keep that line in.'

There is time for a cup of tea and a piece of cake before Les's next appearance so, just for the record, he gives us his definitive versions of a few stories characteristic of North-country humour.

'Two farmers are boasting about how big their vegetables are, and one farmer says, "I bet thee a pint that I've got bigger vegetables than thee." So the other one says, "Nay, tha ain't. Bet thee a pint." So they have this bet and one of the farmers says to his son, "Go to the other farmer and tell him I want to borrow his buzz saw to cut through a turnip." So the son goes off and comes back and says, "You can't have the buzz saw." "Why not?" the farmer asks. "It's stuck in a tattie."

'Another good Northern joke is the one about the fellow lost on the Pennines. The snow's twisting about in the air, he can't see properly and he stumbles blindly on until he comes to this ill-painted door, bangs on it and croaks, "Sanctuary." The door opens and a little girl stands there, soiled pinafore, holding a little rag doll. And he says, "Can I talk to your mummie, luv?" And she says, "Me mum's not here, she's gone out." He says, "Well can I talk to your father?" And she says, "No, me dad's not been in all day." This fellow thinks to himself, "What sort of parents are they that could leave this waif alone in the teeth of a fearsome storm?" And he says, "Don't worry, lass, you're not on your own in this big house any more." And she says, "This isn't the house. It's the lavatory."

'Then there's the joke about the dwarf in a pub, reaching up to take a pint, and a big feller comes in and pushes the dwarf. And the little feller pushes the big feller back, but then falls with a thump, and when he comes round the little feller says, "What did you hit me with?" "The side of me hand – it's a Burmese karate chop to the throat." So the little feller goes out and comes back with a ladder, puts it up the big feller's back, climbs up the ladder and hits him. When the big feller comes round, he says, "What was that?" "A 1939 Austin starting handle."

'Here's a nice daft one. Feller in a pub says, "I know tha face." Other feller says, "Ah don't know thee." "No, but I know thee – never forget a face. I've got it: we were prisoners of war together in Silesia, in a Polish prisoner-of-war camp, and we escaped disguised as nuns on the back of a lorry full of lentils." "No, it wasn't me." "Oh, it'll come to me. I've got it: We sheltered together on Etna when it erupted and we escaped by coming down on cooling lava." "No," says the other feller, "it wasn't me." "Oh, I've got it. We used to go shark wrestling off the Great Barrier Reef and you fell in love with a nympho-maniac pearl diver called Agnes and we fought a duel on the sands for her." "No, it wasn't me." So the feller says, "Were you in the pub last night?" "Yes." "Well, that's where I've seen you."

'You dress them up with language – like this joke, a version of the parrot-dying-in-a-cage joke. There was this feller who bought a marvellous bird in Malaya – a myna bird – and it never said a thing. A friend told him that they need to have things in the cage to keep them entertained – bells, mirrors and so on. So the feller went out and bought them. And the bird still didn't talk. One night he heard a thump and went in, and the bird was on its back in the cage. "What's the matter?" he said. The bird said, "You forgot the bloody ladder."'

Duggie Brown

Duggie Brown is one of the younger brigade of Yorkshire comics. No one, however, has a more common touch. His style is conversational – like that of the lad at the 'do' who has you all in stitches. If he tells a gag, it's woven into his conversation so skilfully as to pass for an anecdote. Like Les Dawson he's verbally zany and vulgar in the true sense of the word. The values and aspirations of his characters are Rotherham through and through. He's cheeky, irreverent and gets away with murder.

I remember taking part in 'Pro-Am Snooker' with him for Yorkshire TV. The presenter was a nice, pleasant chap, very good at his job, who was rather on the short side. He was interviewing Duggie when all of a sudden he was stopped short, mid-question. 'Excuse me,' said Duggie, 'but haven't I seen you on "Fantasy Island"?'

He's a good friend who has appeared in many of my plays, and done me many a favour. He knows the workings of laughter in the North from every side of the spectrum. He should be worth listening to.

Plenty of television work in recent years, including a regular part in the series 'The Enigma Files', has made Duggie Brown's face and personality familiar to people all over the country, so he gets a lot more work outside Yorkshire than he once did. We caught up with him in a Granada Television rehearsal studio in Manchester where one of his fellow actors was a Barnsley comedian so firmly rooted in Yorkshire that he rarely even crosses the border into Lancashire.

Not so Duggie. He reckons that most humour is universal anyway, and even thinks he gets a better response 'down South' because he's a Northerner and a man from Yorkshire. 'There are certain things that won't travel, of course. We've been doing a gag-swapping session today, in between rehearsing, and we realize that if we moved some of the gags down South we just would not get a titter. There's one about Barnsley, for instance. Barnsley is known as "the land of the Chinese rentmen" because when there's a knock on the door, a voice comes from inside: "She ent in." You can't very well transpose that to Watford – "She isn't in [in elegant South-of-England voice]" – it just wouldn't work.

'There's a lovely Northern story which I am now doing in my act which suddenly, even only as far south as Birmingham, doesn't get a laugh. It's about two lads who are swinging on the garden gate. They are about nine years old, live in Sheffield, or wherever. One of them says, "Tell me, if tha were king of England, what would tha do?" "Well," says the second lad, "ah'd eat bacon butties all day and ah'd swing back and forwards on t'gate. Why, what would tha do?" And this other little laddie swings backwards and forwards and his friend says, "Tha's taking a long time," and he answers, "Well, tha's mentioned two best things already."

'You don't get the instant response to that down South, but in Yorkshire it's lovely.

'Here's another nice one, which sometimes I get away with down South or even up in Scotland. Chap takes his cat to the vet to have it immunized because he's going to take it abroad, you see, and the vet says to him, "Is the cat a tom?" and he says, "No, I brought it with me."' (Didn't get it? 'A tom' when spoken with a Northern accent sounds like 'at home'.)

Duggie has never analyzed what he does or why it goes down well. He reckons that humour, or the response to it, is the security of people watching someone who is either confident or enjoying himself. 'If you go to Blackpool, to the big Pleasure Beach there, the first thing you see when you go in is the great enormous clown in the cage. The clown just laughs all day, and people just stand there watching him. He's not saying any gags, he's just waddling about laughing, and people laugh with him. Humour's infectious to the extent that if people see that you are enjoying yourself, even though you might be making a mess of it – and I've done that sometimes – if you get out of it in a nice way they are secure in what you are doing.

31

'Les Dawson, for instance. I love Les because he has great confidence in what he is doing. It's that security thing. I've been to some places where the audiences won't laugh because the building is wrong around them, the hotel is wrong and the entertainer feels out of place. But Les makes you feel that you are sitting at home in his own house.

'There are comics and comedians. A comedian says funny things, a comic says things funny. Tommy Copper is a comic, I hope I am a comic. Bob Monkhouse is a comedian, relying on the strength of the words he is delivering. I rely on how I am going over and how I am feeling in myself. I do the oldest gags going. There's a parrot gag that has been going for years and years and I have made it my own now, with variations. The basic gag is the parrot and the plumber, which I don't do now because lots of others do it. I even heard it again on 'The Comedians' quite recently. I do a variation which is a good one, if you know the original joke – it goes like this:

'There was a fellow whose speciality was growing fruit, which he wanted for a big show in London. He had a greenhouse in which he grew enormous tomatoes and enormous bananas, enormous apples, and beautiful big plums. One day, there was a flash of lightning which hit his greenhouse and destroyed all his fruit. He was in despair. He was in the pub, and this man came up and said, "What's the matter?" and he said, "Well, you know I've been preparing my fruit for London, especially the plums, and the lightning's just split all the skins and everything." And the man said, "Oh dear. Well, don't worry, there's a man who lives on the corner of our street and actually his hobby is that he can do things with fruit – he repairs them." "Is it his hobby, or is it his job?" "It's his hobby. His job is playing the bagpipes in the Scots Guards. Go round and see him." So the fellow went round and knocked on the door, but he wasn't there. So he left a message saying he wanted all his fruit looked after. Later the bagpipe player came to his house and knocked on the door. And the fellow said, "Who is it?" and he replied, "It's the piper, I've come to mend your plums."

'The original parrot joke was broadcast on the very first 'Comedians' in 1971 and is on the original record. I got twenty-seven laughs in the one tag line.'

Duggie Brown started off his career as a guitar player. He had been working abroad a lot for the Americans in Greece, Turkey and France, and started doing patter. He was putting about twenty-five minutes of patter between the guitar playing and songs when he suddenly realized it would be better for him to be doing patter because comedy was paid more at that time. Duggie thought he might as well be doing it for himself as for the three other fellows in the group, so he left them. He did a lot of variety in Scotland and was Frank Castle's straight man. 'Frank always says, "The only reason you took to comedy was because I make it look so easy." That's his famous line.'

Duggie settled back in Rotherham when he realized that he wanted his little daughter to be educated in Yorkshire rather than in Scotland where they were living. Down in Rotherham he started going out with a double act called Bob and Jack Young – Bob is now Robert Young, a very well-known tenor.

Fate nodded in Duggie's direction one night when he gave them a lift to Doncaster and the other act sharing the bill with the Youngs did not turn up. 'The guy there said, "Why don't you get up and sing a couple of songs?" and I did and told gags in between. I went back again, and gradually the gags took over and now the guitar's gone and it's all comedy.'

He writes a lot of his own material, especially the topical stuff. Unlike many comics, he likes topical material. Football, politics, anything that has happened that day can provide material for the evening's work. 'I did one story during the petrol strike which grew out of something that happened to me. I was on the M5 going down to Bristol and in one of the service areas there was a sign where you pulled in which said: "Maximum £3 and minimum £2". I didn't really know what they were trying to prove. That night I used it in a gag: there was an Irish fellow in front of me in the petrol queue and he gave the chap £8 and said, "Can I have the maximum twice and the minimum once." That one got a lovely round of applause.

'People don't laugh at topical gags. They laugh at the hoary old ones, but they applaud topical ones. Ted Rodgers gets a lot of applause at the end of his act, but not a lot of laughter.'

On the whole, Duggie is not worried about the effect appearing on television has on his club and stage work. 'When that old parrot gag went out of the routine, people used to come and request it. Only recently I nearly ended up with a terrible row over it. I walked out on stage and a woman kept shouting, "Tell the parrot gag, tell the parrot gag." If they ask you for the parrot gag, then they know it, and so they know the tag line. It's like requesting Tom Jones to sing "Delilah". Anyway, the woman was a bit . . . she'd had a few. Her husband was on her side, getting her to argue with me, you know. I did not want to do it because I could only do it once the way I did it on television – pretending to forget it – because after that it was too well known; the point was lost.

'Remember Charlie Williams? He had a bad time on "The Golden Shot". It's five years and more ago now, but people still say to me, "Well, how's Ron Goodman?" "Fine." "Shame about Charlie, wasn't it?" – as if it happened only recently.

Charlie's still working a lot, got his nice big Rolls-Royce and what-not, but people did see his Achilles heel in that programme. If you have to handle hecklers and they can get back at you, then you are lost. You've no answer to it.

'On the other hand, television can be a help with your club work. If people are requesting jokes they have seen on telly, then you have already got something going with them. I did a gag about a chap with a cleft palate which went on and on, and people requested that, so it doesn't really matter about giving your material an airing on telly. If people have come to a club and brought a few friends with them, and request a gag, they can nudge their friends, give them the elbow, and say, "Oh, this is a good one, wait till you hear this one." They feel secure, and it's a fact that whatever's happening to the person in the gag, the reason the listener laughs is because he's happy it's not happening to him. Cleft palate, people being blown up, run over by steamrollers, or whatever, the initial laughter comes because of the feeling "Thank God, it's not me." And, of course, seeing somebody – me – enjoying themselves is the main thing.

'Being on television can be a definite help sometimes, too. On stage, I can take the mickey out of what I've done for television. When I was in "The Enigma Files", my sister was in "Coronation Street" and I had just done the "Pro-Celebrity Snooker" thing, so my opening line after all that was, "Well, I don't know if I'm a comedian, a detective, a snooker player or a drag artist from 'Coronation Street'," which round this area got a laugh because there's a lot of interest in the two of us.'

Duggie did not have any kind of theatrical childhood, so it is surprising that he, his sister and his brother should all have found their way into the entertainment business. His elder brother has just started compèring all the rugby shows in Zambia, where he lives.

'My father was a bricklayer and me mum a housewife. We never went to variety theatre when I was a kid. I remember going down to the Regent Theatre in Birmingham in 1952, when I was twelve. I did my first show there – a fieldmouse in *Toad of Toad Hall*. And I just got the bug.

'With my father being in the steelworks, and my brother,

when I left school I went there too. I was getting £4 7s 6d a week, had holes in my jeans, and was breathing in horrible fumes. But when I had left school I'd also joined a skiffle group. Its lead guitar was Stan Crowther, now Rotherham's MP, and I don't know that he isn't a bigger comic than I am. I was getting thirty bob for playing in the skiffle group on a Friday night and I thought, "There's something wrong here. I enjoy doing this and I don't enjoy the other, so I'll become a professional." The big thing then was, "Are you a professional?" Well, we got three weeks' work – a week at Collin's Islington Music Hall in London, a week at City Varieties in Leeds, and then the Middlesbrough Empire – all spread over a year, but on the strength of those three weeks I said, "I'm a pro."

'I became Duggie Brown gradually. My middle name is Douglas and the group's drummer was called Bill Brown. We called ourselves the Four Imps when we did "6.5 Special", which Jim Dale was compèring at that time. Then we became the Four Kool Katz, but that didn't seem right in those nice posh hotels with the cabaret act. We wanted something like the Hedley Ward Trio, so round about 1959–60 we became the Douglas Brown Four. When I left the group I became a singer called Douglas-Browne – hyphenated and with an "e" on the end. I've still got cards to prove it – and my address was 31 Plum Tree Caravan Site. The hyphen was dropped first, then the "e", then Douglas became Duggie.'

Like everything else, the Northern clubs and theatres are in a bit of a bad way at present – 'People aren't going to pay six quid to see me when they saw me in Wakefield Working-men's Club two years ago for two quid' – but, even so, it is still the clubs which help comedy thrive in the North. 'We have the outlets here. Down South, you have the theatre, where Max Miller and the like developed. But up here you have the working-men's clubs, which are outlets for people to go and try themselves out, to find out if they really are funny. Where would they go and do that in London?

'At one time in London you could work fifty-two weeks of the year, each week in a different theatre. Now they have all gone and nothing's replaced them. Up here, there are even the factory clubs, which are beautiful to work. Out at Hayes, near Manchester Airport, there are several good clubs, so you can go and try it at one place, and if you die on your backside, you can go back to the drawing board and, if you dare, you can try it again at another place nearby without it costing you a lot in petrol.

'And, of course, there is a great tradition here too. I used to be compère at Batley Variety Club. One night they had Johnny Mathis making his second appearance there; there was me – and I was on "The Comedians" as well – there were Little and Large, six girl dancers, a magic juggling act, a girl singer and a fourteen-piece orchestra, all in the first half of the show. I always remember, about the third night, a bloke standing at the bar and saying, "He's not as good as he used to be, is he?" – and that was Johnny Mathis, and it was £2.50 to get in. I mean, to see Johnny Mathis, even at that time, would have been at least £10 or £12 in London. Audiences get spoiled.'

Duggie says it with a certain pride. They are his kind of people, and he enjoys spoiling them.

Eric and Ernie

Eric and Ernie are without doubt our most popular Northern comedians. They've perfected the Northern insult: witness this in their treatment of Des O'Connor. Good-natured rudeness is now accepted almost universally. They never stop, on or off the stage – you're never safe when in their company.

I remember bumping into them in the foyer of the BBC TV Centre. They were very nice, even serious, asking me always to consider them if I ever had an idea for a straight play which involved their type. Like all comedians they want to go serious now and then, and I said I'd always bear them in mind. I felt flattered as the place was packed with visitors, many of them staring at me chinwagging with the famous pair on such intimate terms. I should have known better: as I was walking away from them towards the door, Eric demanded, for all to hear, '*Who* is he?' It was Ernie's cue to reply, 'I thought *you* knew him!' to which came the rejoinder, '*I* don't know who he is. Flaming cheek!'

So much has been written about them – let them speak for themselves. Here is a part of a television script specially written for them by Eddie Braben. For me it says all there is to say about their special brand of humour.

Our heroes are discovered sitting up in bed. It is Saturday night, and Ernie is writing – probably the Great Play.

Eric: Sunday tomorrow. Have a lie-in.

Ernie: Won't be much of a lie-in, if they're back again tomorrow morning.

Eric: Who?

Ernie: Salvation Army.

Eric: I like the Salvation Army. Wouldn't be Sunday without them.

Ernie: My father used to play in the Salvation Army band. Played the cornet.

Eric: I remember your dad in the Salvation Army. He suited that bonnet. I must be honest, Ern – your dad could play that cornet.

Ernie: I'll say.

Eric: The band used to meet every Sunday morning on the corner of Tarryassan Street.

Ernie: Outside the bread shop.

Eric: Hundreds waiting for your dad to ride up on his bike.

Ernie: Nobody could play 'Onward Christian Soldiers' like my dad.

Eric: It's the only time I've ever seen people dancing to 'Onward Christian Soldiers'.

Ernie: They used to call my dad the Harry James of Tarryassan Street.

Eric: And that was no understatement. Remember that Sunday he was so keen to play he forgot to take his bicycle clips off?

Ernie: Yes.

Eric: Took four days for his knee caps to go down.

Ernie: Oh, very funny! What about your father?

Eric: What about my father?

Ernie: I never saw him sober.

Eric: It was his outlet, wasn't it?

Ernie: What do you mean – his outlet?

Eric: From the toils of it – the toils of the week.

Ernie: Toils of the week! He was on the dole for twelve years. At the Labour Exchange they even named a cubicle after him.

Eric: He's a tax exile now, my dad.

Ernie: Your dad a tax exile!

Eric: He's in prison.

Ernie: Anyway, you couldn't show respect on a Sunday because you had to earn a few bob delivering newspapers.

Eric: No shame in that.

Ernie: While me and mine were showing respect.

Eric: Don't forget I went to your house to deliver the papers on Sunday.

Ernie: I know that.

Eric: Your dad waiting for me by the front gate so's he could hide the *News of the World* under his raincoat.

Ernie: We were a good-living family.

Eric: I know. Your mother wanted you to be a nun.

Ernie: My dad made sure I went to Sunday school every week.

Eric: There was a reason.

Ernie: Reason? What do you mean?

Eric: You know . . . [nudges Ernie]

Ernie: No, I don't. What was the reason?

Eric: So as he could polish his cornet in peace.

Ernie: Oh. I didn't really want to go to Sunday school.

Eric: Not many lads do when they are twenty-three.

Ernie: You can mock. A good-living family we were. In church we had our own special pew.

Eric: That's why nobody sat near you.

Ernie: I can see me and my mother now singing 'Abide With Me'.

Eric: Only when she took in lodgers.

Ernie: Respectable family, we were. Can't remember you going to Sunday school.

Eric: I did.

Ernie: Once a year at Christmas for the free orange. Lived a full childhood, I did.

Eric: You still are.

Ernie: I was in the Cubs. I remember marching at the head of the pack on Empire Day. With the wolf's head on the pole.

Eric: Is that what is was? I thought it was your dad keeping an eye on you.

Ernie: Full uniform, I had. You couldn't afford the full uniform. All you had was two green ribbons hanging from your stocking tops.

Eric: I was a good Cub, I was. I remember what it was all about. I could light a fire without matches – if it was electric.

Ernie: You were hopeless in the Cubs – hopeless! Couldn't do a thing.

Eric: Who?

Ernie: You.

Eric: Oh? Give us your leg then.

Ernie: What do you want my leg for?

Eric: I'll tie a sheepshank in it.

Fadeout

Bobby Thompson

Mentioning this book to people I've met casually, while just hopping around, going about my business, I've been amazed at the fund of memories there are about the North and its comedians. Paul Daniels, the man of magic of the moment, believes like many others that it was the social deprivation and the interdependence of people that gave birth to traditional Northern humour. 'But,' I asked, 'why not South Wales, for instance – nowhere could you find a more close-knit working-class community, yet they have no such tradition of humour, not on the scale of the North at any rate.' His answer was interesting. 'They don't talk right,' he said. 'You can't crack gags with a sing-song voice. Wax cynical, yes, but be wise-cracking funny, no.'

And this led us on to . . . Bobby Thompson. If you are from anywhere but the North-East, you'll now be asking, 'Who?' Well, this man has been the most popular stand-up comedian in Newcastle and its surrounds for the past twenty or thirty years. His esoteric, quick-fire, guttural, choking delivery is tailor-made for gags – if only you can understand what he's saying. Alan Price raves about him, as does Jack Charlton. Lawrie McMenemy plays Bobby Thompson tapés in his car, and can tell you Bobby Thompson stories in his own authentic Geordie accent by the hour.

The rest of the country is now beginning to notice him. He even made it to the *Observer Magazine* not long ago, in a profile by Richard Kelly. What follows is mostly Mr Kelly's interview, with a few Bobby Thompson stories, as recollected by Lawrie McMenemy, added to illustrate how this great comedian makes his fellow Geordies laugh.

Bobby Thompson is now what he has always been – a survivor for whom luxury is not so much accessible as irrelevant and for whom home comforts are the only reality. He is a veteran of the seige economy, buffeted by depression and war, and striving, with some success, to avoid the sharper edges of each. He meets the taunts of fecklessness, improvidence and irresponsibility ('He'll neither work nor want'), launched at him and his kind by the self-righteous and respectable, with the imperishable slogan, 'Sup up, lads, poverty's no disgrace' (though he himself has been teetotal for the past thirteen years).

To the respectable section of the working class, the eighth and most deadly of all sins is debt. Not so to Bobby. To the television interviewer who suggests that the bad old days are coming back again, 'There's plenty of money about,' he replies dismissively. 'Look at the amount we owe.' No longer true in his case, of course, but the point is taken. He can look hard-nosed at the women in the audience and weigh up how much debt they are carrying. 'This would be a nudist camp if all the women took the

41

catalogue stuff off,' he says, referring to the mail-order transactions which have replaced the old money clubs in the colliery villages.

Success of the runaway kind has come to this little, slightly built man ('six and a half stone wet through') after a life of ups and downs. Recently at the age of seventy, he signed a contract to appear in pantomime at £2,500 a week for seven weeks, doing a single spot lasting twenty-five minutes at each performance. His first long-playing record, 'The Little Waster', sold over 120,000 copies in the year it was issued, and brought him in some £33,000 in royalties. Nobody is more surprised at its success than Bobby himself. Woolworths put in an initial order for 25 copies, which were sold within the hour, and placed a repeat order for 5,000. When these too were exhausted, the local branch manager came knocking on Bobby's door for more.

Born at New Penshaw in the heart of the north-east Durham coalfield, Bobby left school at fourteen and, like his father and three brothers, went straight down the pit. The colliery closed down when he was twenty and, left without work, he joined a concert party. In 1934 he made his first broadcast from the BBC's Newcastle studios in a programme called 'Pit People', featuring 'Billy Bankhead's Mouth Organ Band with Bobby Thompson, Comedian'.

After the outbreak of war Bobby was called up into the Border Regiment and stationed at Carlisle. In his act, and on his record, he does an army sequence, making a bedraggled appearance in ill-fitting battledress and filthy forage cap as the band plays 'Bladon Races'. The audience bursts into laughter before he even opens his mouth. As the laughter subsides he fixes them censoriously with his one good eye (he lost the other playing cricket at fourteen) and with mock indignation shouts, 'You never laughed at me when I was fighting for you.'

His wartime sequence contains the nearest thing to a dirty joke in his whole act. He goes on about how he had to go into the army and did not want to. He had to leave behind his wife – a giant of a woman, and he's just a skinny little man. He relates how he wrote to his wife from camp when he'd been in only three days: 'My darling, dear Bella, I'm missing you very very badly and I do not like it here; I wish I was home.' And in three days, back came a letter: 'Dear little Bobby, thank you for your letter' – and there was £2 in it, which was a fortune to him in those days. So he wrote a better letter the next week, and back came another £2. Then he thought, 'There's a rabbit off here somewhere' [traditional Geordie saying, meaning 'I smell a rat'], and asked for compassionate leave to go home, telling the sergeant his wife was having a baby. When he got home, a big Yank opened the door and said, 'Hullo, who are you?' And Bobby replied, 'I'm little Bobby. Who are you?' – to which the Yank answered, 'I'm the one who's sending you £2 a week.' (And, Bobby tells his audience, when he got back to camp the Sergeant asked him if it was a boy or a girl, and he replied 'Oh, it takes a long time!')

The wartime sequence also includes a long, rambling telephone conversation with Mrs Neville Chamberlain. He was on his local Street Committee at the time ('I was chairman; I wanted to be treasurer, but they all knew about me') and one day one of the committee asked him if he had heard there was going to be a war. No, Bobby hadn't heard, so – very matter of fact – 'I rang Neville Chamberlain and his missus, Bertha, answered. Oh, she doesn't half talk funny. And she says [very posh], "Helloo, wha's speaking?" And I said, "Little Bobby Thompson." "Oh, hang on a minute, Bobby, I've got a pan of chips on." So she goes in the back, comes back to the phone and says "Whit can I do for you?" "Is Neville in?" "Oh, he's just doon gittin' the coal ..."' It is a long monologue, very humorous, bringing people down to earth, and Bobby's audience love it. After all, why shouldn't Mrs Chamberlain have a pan of chips on, why shouldn't Mr Chamberlain be getting the coal up?

Shortly after the war, Bobby's big break came with the long-running radio series from the North-East, 'Wot Cheor, Geordie'. From the outset it was obvious that here was an original. He was, and still is, himself, on or off stage. 'I'm no star,' he says, 'I'm just an ordinary man. I mix with the local lads every day at the bookie's shop and that's where I hear the stories.' He transmits scenes and conversations from pit and

43

club life in the Durham coalfield with uncanny accuracy. Although it excluded his comic appearance, radio was to prove the ideal vehicle for his talent. He introduced a whole range of characters: his mother-in-law, forever blackguarding the waster her daughter married, the soppy brother-in-law, the authoritarian colliery manager and his 'wife', a strident harpy.

His biggest laugh, he recalls, was in a performance of 'Wot Cheor, Geordie' at the Miners' Welfare Hall, Ferryhill, County Durham, in the heart of the Labour homelands. It was in the early 1950s when the big election issue was the provision of free dentures, wigs and other appliances under the National Health Service, some of which the Conservatives were pledged to revoke. Bobby carefully set the scene in the club on the day following the election, with Conservative gains coming over the radio every minute and his slow-witted father-in-law devouring the racing news, spectacles on the end of his nose, and slowly dozing off under the influence of his second or third pint. At three o'clock the club steward calls time. 'Howway, lads,' he shouts. 'Let's have your glasses.' The old man wakes up suddenly. 'Yer bugger,' he says, 'is the Tories back already?' The effect on the audience was electrifying. Pandemonium broke loose, shrieks of laughter interspersed with shouting and cheering, made up in equal parts of defiance and derision. This is what total identification means, and this is Bobby's secret.

When commercial television reached the North-East, Bobby was understandably attracted to the new medium (he is, after all, a visual as well as an aural comedian) and signed up for a series with the new Tyne Tees company. It was an unqualified disaster. He was criticized, according to him, for being too 'localified' by a producer – his contract was not renewed.

The Little Waster, as the 'wife' in his act always described him, was back to the lean times again. From having topped the bill in every major North-East theatre, he was reduced to entering go-as-you-please competitions for £3 or £4 if he was lucky. Then his wife in real life died, a loss both emotionally and as a support for his act. With two young children to look after, he gave up the drink and had the luck to fall in with a good agent.

Today the bank manager invites him out to lunch and asks

him if there are any companies in which he would like to invest. But he is not taking any chances. The companies, he says, might go defunct 'like I did'. 'You never forget when you had nowt,' he reflects, remembering the shifts and evasions which enabled him to survive the poverty of the pit village, the very antics which earned him the almost endearing title of the Little Waster. In the affluent society of today, or what is left of it, he can see little cause for complaint. 'When I was a lad, you used to wear your Sunday suit on a Sunday, not through the week, but now, if they get a full week's work in, they're away to buy a set of golf clubs.'

Dave Morris

I barely remember Dave Morris. I think he was in *Radio Fun*, that smashing little comic we used to read when we were kids. But wherever I've been, and mentioned this book, the cry has gone up: 'You must have Dave Morris in it.' I can see him clearly in my mind's eye – his big round face and straw hat, his horn-rims, and throaty rasp of a voice; I remember the successful 'Club Night' on the radio, a forerunner of so many contemporary comedy shows. The producer of a number of these, John Ammonds, was also the 'Club Night' producer in his early days. So who better to tell us about Dave and his own particular brand of Northern comedy than John himself.

If you did not know better, you would assume that Dave Morris had been a successful music-hall and club performer before he achieved recognition as a radio comedy star. After all, most people who are old enough to remember him at all have a good picture of him in their minds, suggesting that his was an all-round personality, with a face and figure as well as a voice. In fact, according to John Ammonds, Morris made only one journey south to that music hall Mecca, the London Palladium, and was – if rumour speaks truth – paid off on the Monday night.

David Morris died in the early 1960s, before his television career had a chance really to take off, so it is for his radio work that he is best remembered, and for his annual summer season

45

at Blackpool, where he used to play to capacity audiences with his 'Club Night' show. In Blackpool, where he lived, he built a repertory company around him of people who were seldom pro actors. He had people like an ex-miner and a former lorry driver playing important parts in his show. He once tried to get the impressario Emile Littler to pay the salary of one of them, Joe Gladwyn, the lorry driver, whom Dave wanted to appear in a panto season with him at the Ardwick Hippodrome. Mr Littler, who had taken on Morris only, wrote back, 'Certainly not. In any case I've never heard of him.' To which Dave Morris replied, 'Dear Mr Littler, I have shown your letter to Joe Gladwyn, and as a point of interest, Joe Gladwyn has never heard of you.' It was the sort of zany correspondence to be expected of a comedian who used to send his scripts to the BBC secretary for typing in 12-foot-long rolls, and even on occasion

addressed them to the BBC, c/o Lewis's Arcade – a notorious prostitutes' pick-up place in Manchester in those days.

'Club Night' was first broadcast in the early fifties. Its setting was a typical working-men's club of the period, a much more modest affair than the great Northern clubs of the following two decades, which usually offered a programme of a few acts and a musical item or two. The radio show followed this scheme, with one major difference: it allowed its audience backstage, as it were, to hear the club's committee in action. Morris's role was that of a sort of English Sergeant Bilko; he was the committee member who always managed to worm his way into the job of club treasurer, mainly so that he could divert the club's funds and beer to his own use or advantage. He used a stooge, partly to help get the laughs, but also because he was so short-sighted that he could not read his scripts and had to memorize them. If his memory went blank for a vital second or two on radio, the stooge could step in with a couple of lines to help him over the gap.

He liked to use catch phrases as familiar landmarks in his shows. He always had a topical line at the beginning, like 'What a welcome, what a reception; just like Winston Churchill at the Kremlin.' And he would include some incident which would allow him to say, 'I suppose the whole thing was hushed up.' For example, there was the time when the county-voiced newsreader Roger Moffat appeared on 'Club Night' with a story of how he had been reading the news when something terrible happened. 'I was reading the football results and I read, "Accrington Stanley 2," then I turned over two pages at once and read, "Marilyn Monroe 3."' 'Oh, how terrible,' said Dave, dramatizing the incident. 'I suppose the whole thing was hushed up.'

Most people in the business remember Dave Morris's command of words as his greatest asset. John Ammonds can happily reminisce for hours about the joys of working with him. He says that Dave Morris thought of himself as appealing to the cloth-cap audience, whereas in reality his humour, and the way he expressed it, was very like that of Groucho Marx and even had Monty Python-type overtones of mad surrealism.

Take, for instance, Dave's stories of his army life. In 'Club Night' he would be in the club's bar, telling anyone who would listen about his career in the Cheshire Regiment. This, according to Dave, was the only regiment in the British Army privileged to march through Accrington carrying their horses at the slope. Or there was the Scunthorpe Highland Light Infantry, which was the only regiment granted the privilege – the very rare privilege – of marching through Scunthorpe two men to a kilt. And what about the Punjab Rifles? They were allowed to carry their elephants at the slope through Liverpool . . . and so on. The Goons would have loved it, just as the radio audiences loved such stories as the one in which the regimental sergeant major announced that the regiment was going to celebrate the night the regimental goat had twins: they'd been calling it Billy for years.

Many of Dave's stories round the bar were on the lines of: 'Did I ever tell you about the time I became . . .' – for example, when he 'became' a tourist guide in London. John Ammonds remembers the story word for word: 'I was a guide at the Tower of London and it was my job to show people round, and I used to say, "This place, ladies and gentlemen, was the spot where they beheaded Mary, Queen of Scots. And, if you remember, before she died she uttered those immortal words, 'When I die and you open me up, there on my heart will be engraved "Skegness Is So Bracing."'"' It is the gloriously daft combination of wildly inaccurate history with the words on a British Railways poster that John Ammonds savours.

Then there was the occasion when Dave 'became' a barrister. 'In my first case as a barrister I was defending a man on two charges – capital murder and having his chimney on fire. I got him off the murder charge, but they hanged him for having his chimney on fire. I appealed, but lost the appeal and they hanged him again the following Friday.'

Dave's 'career' as a teaplanter was not uneventful either. 'I used to sit on the verandah at sunset, smoking a final rickshaw . . .' 'What!' cried his stooge, 'that's a carriage!' 'Yes, and those rubber wheels are a terrible smoke.'

In one of his 'careers', Dave got into a spot of bother. 'When

48

cornered, I did the only thing I could do – turned my hat round backwards, put my coat on inside out, gave a wrong name and walked away.'

The thing that John Ammonds remembers best about all these stories is the great conviction with which they were told. Even when just rehearsing the radio series, Dave would give each line everything he had, even leaning across the rehearsal-room table to put his point to the actor concerned. There was, for instance, a scene in 'Club Night' when a Southerner, just moved up North, asked, 'What have you got in the North of England? You've got no entertainment, you've got no night life.' Dave was horrified. 'No night life in the North of England?' He paused, leaned forward so that his face came right up to the other actor's and said, sincerely and impressively, 'There's a cabman's shelter in Accrington where you get get pies, peas and chips until three o'clock in the morning.'

Arthur Askey, George Formby and Gracie Fields

Arthur Askey and George Formby, together with Frank Randle, are my childhood laughter – encapsulated. Their radio shows and films remain indestructable in the well of my memory. All I have to do is dip down and pluck out a chuckle.

I met Arthur and 'Stinker' Murdoch a couple of years ago and told them of my memories of 'Bandwagon' and Mrs Bagwash and her daughter Nausea. They were delighted to talk about them with me. I take my kids to see Arthur now, still as sprightly as ever, in the local panto. Here are some memories of Arthur, George and, of course, good old Gracie Fields (they all came from 'around my way'), taken from their published life stories.

One of the funniest stories in big-hearted Arthur's auto-biography, *Before Your Very Eyes*, concerned him and Richard Murdoch in Liverpool. They were on tour in 1939, and as part of their contract had to appear in a major store which sold Symington's products in every town they visited.

So when we arrived in Liverpool, we were advertised to do

our stint at Coopers in Church Street. The streets around the store were alive with people, while inside the shop was crammed to the doors. With a police escort, Dickie and I were smuggled in through a back door and taken up to the fourth floor in a lift that was usually used to carry sacks of flour. We appeared to cheers and rounds of applause and, as usual, climbed on to the counter where hundreds of tins of Symington's soups were piled up in pyramids 6 feet high. The adoring throng kept up the cheers and applause until eventually I quelled the mob and took a deep breath to deliver my blessing, when a bowler hat (that was all I could see of him) in the second row shouted, 'When are you coming to see your Aunt Cis?' It was my Uncle Charlie who had obviously been celebrating his nephew's success. Dickie Murdoch laughed so much that he knocked over all the tins and then fell off the counter backwards.

Arthur's mum stars in another story about the early life of the great star:

I had been at Kinmel (army camp) only a few hours when my parents turned up. They were, ostensibly, on their holidays, but really wanted to be near their warrior son. I managed to scrounge a pass and walked with them from the camp to their hotel. My mother had taken my arm, and I was smoking a cigarette, when I noticed an officer approaching. As we passed, I gave him a very smart salute which he acknowledged by shouting, 'Take that cigarette out of your mouth when you salute an officer!' My mother swung round and replied with equal ferocity, 'You leave my boy alone – he didn't want to join in the first place!' We did not stay long at Kinmel, for we were soon posted to the Far East – Great Yarmouth.

Askey's autobiography is full of one-line gags like the last one in the above story, no doubt a legacy from his days with pier-end concert parties where he used to have a big success with lines like (to the people sitting on the wooden-slatted sixpenny seats):

'Whatever you think of the show, you will always go away with the same impression!' Then there's the gag about the house in which he was born in Liverpool: 'They've got a plaque on the wall that tells the whole romantic legend in one word – "Condemned!" And a self-put-down from the former Liverpool Cathedral choirboy: 'When war broke out, I was frequently asked if I would sing to the wounded soldiers – as if they hadn't suffered enough!'

He quotes a whole string of waiter jokes he was asked to produce for a scene in his first film. They all ended up on the cutting-room floor, which seems a shame:

'Waiter, do you serve lobsters?'
'Yes, sir, sit down – we serve anybody.'

'I'm so hungry I could eat a horse.'
'We've only got the doovers.'
'What doovers?'
'The horse's doovers.'

'Have you any fresh salmon?'
'I think it will be fresh, sir!'
'What do you mean, you think it will be fresh?'
'Well, we don't know until we open the tin!'

'Have you a wild duck?'
'No, sir, but I've got a tame one I could aggravate for you.'

Every one a little gem! And there's a lot more of the same. It's good to know that the author of them is still hard at work bringing pleasure to television viewers by the million.

I did not much enjoy the rather sad biography they produced about George Formby, but there was one funny story which encapsulates very neatly his throw-away Northern style:

Tommy Trinder remembers going to Beryldene and being shown the newly decorated Chinese room. Chinese writing ran down the sides of the fireplace. 'What's it say?' he asked. In earnest, George replied, 'This side says "Beryl" and that side says "George".' 'Who did it?' said Tommy. 'Ooh, some local builder,' was George's answer.

Gracie Fields wrote a splendidly funny, honest and down-to-earth autobiography, called *Sing As We Go*, in which her family played major roles. Not for our Gracie the sort of autobiography in which everyone appears larger than life and twice as important. Her family were ordinary folk from Rochdale, and not even the enormous success of their Grace was going to change that. Take their view of her villa on Capri, for instance. Here, from *Sing As We Go*, is how it was described to Monty Banks, who became Grace's second husband:

''Ave you seen our Grace's place over there?' Dad demanded.

Monty shook his head. Dad grunted and Mum folded her hands primly. 'It's very nice,' she said stoutly.

'Nice!' roared Dad, launching into the tale. 'First of all she goes and buys half a blasted mountain, then she carts me over there to see that it gets knocked down. You can't make them I-talians understand Lancashire, you know,' he continued to Italian-born Monty. 'Forty of 'em she had working out there all summer. I give 'em a job to do, and when I turn round they've all gone fishing, or swimming, or drinking that *vino*. I had to lug all them stones about myself, put new windows in the place, and build a path to get to it . . . crazy blasted place . . .' He paused, and then looked sorrowfully at Monty. 'All t'summer I were there,' he said again, 'and not one good mug of beer in the whole place.'

Mum frowned impatiently, but had to add her bit. 'I must say I don't like that Vesuvius being so near,' she said. 'Everything look like it's crumbling down to me. But I did teach the woman over there how to make good Yorkshire pudding and happen it won't be so bad when we go over again.'

'When you get there,' sister Betty chimed in, 'you have to drive to Grace's place in carriages. Honestly, Monty, with me Mumma and Dad stuck up there in front, and all of us following along behind in pairs, we look like a ruddy Roman chariot race.'

Edith completed the picture of my Capri paradise for Monty. 'I said to our Grace when I got there,' she said wistfully. ' "Why on earth couldn't you have picked somewhere really nice, nearer home, like Bournemouth or Southport?" '

Before Capri, there had been a house called Peacehaven near Brighton, to which most of the family went at weekends. Every time we found that Mum had been visiting the neighbours during the week. 'Ee, they've got a lovely garden path, Grace, you must come and see it.'

'Yes, Mumma, it is lovely, but we've *got* a lovely garden path. New. Hardly walked on.'

'Aye; but it's not as nice as their.'

Next time I'd go down there'd be a new path, just like the neighbours'.'

'We ought to have a tennis court, Grace,' said Mum firmly.

'No, Mumma, none of us plays tennis.'

We got the tennis court. Dad kept his chickens on it. Then Mum saw someone's goldfish pond. 'Ah'll make one like that myself,' said Dad.

Next time I arrived he led me to the top of the garden. 'Ah got carried away,' he explained, peering down the gaping great cavern in front of us. 'It went proper deep.'

'Deep enough for a swimming pool,' said Jenny.

We made it into a swimming pool. Then we got terrified that the babies would fall in, so we filled it up with muck. It stayed that way till one hot summer's day when someone said they must have a swim, so we heaved all the muck out again, and put a boat on the water. I was sitting by the pool, all fancy on a chaise-longue with my feet up, when Dad arrived home from the pub full of beer and benevolence and beamed at me: 'This is the life, Grace! Ooo-ho! a life on the ocean wave!' He put one foot in the boat and sank base over apex to the bottom. I had to jump in with all my clothes on to rescue him. After that we had rails and a couple of lifebelts put around our private ocean, and it was never warm enough to go swimming in it again.

One of the nicest things about Gracie was that she never became grand, whatever the heights to which her career might take her. She did not like her Rolls Royce: it felt like going to work in a hearse. She did like shopping in Woolworths but had to stop doing that because the crowds gathered round her got so big they had to call the police. And she did like breaking her bread into her soup.

> I went to one big dinner one night, and saw the host, a Lord Somebody, breaking up his bread and putting it in his soup. I was so astonished that I blurted out, 'They told me never to do that, but *you're* doing it!' He was sensible that chap. 'Good Lord, don't mind what "they" say,' he told me. 'If you like bread in your soup, and I do, put the blasted bread in.' I put the blasted bread in. It seemed easy after that. I've done it ever since.

Even when the Inland Revenue were after her, and she had to sell her London house to pay her income tax, she kept her sense of proportion – and her North-country frugality. She still had her voice, the Inland Revenue couldn't take that; nor, if she had anything to do with it, were they going to get the goldfish and the tiger lilies in the garden of the London house. In the dead of night, she went back to the house, scooped every goldfish out of the pond, and dug up all her tiger lilies.

You can't keep a good lass down.

The New Wave

In the early sixties a cultural revolution took place, particularly in my profession, releasing a flood of talent from the Northern Counties of England. Its most important aspect was the throwing-over of repressive Southern or metropolitan-based *mores* in speech and behaviour, which allowed young people of my generation in particular to relax and have confidence in and exploit their essential Northernness.

Actors like Albert Finney and Tom Courtenay were able to inject a new vitality into British films, TV and theatre, using the works of a veritable flood tide of Northern playwrights: Keith Waterhouse, Willis Hall, Henry Livings, Alan Plater, Alan Prior, Stan Barstow and many others suddenly found that their ethnic cries of protest or celebration were regarded as legitimate – no more were individuals called upon to submerge their buoyancy and good raw sense in the wishy-washy world of South Ken. in order to be taken seriously. Soon we were to have our flat vowels accepted universally – on television, in Parliament, even in Downing Street. The North was discovered to be a refreshing, stimulating and prolific launching-pad for talented people in all walks of life.

What do those who found success on the crest of that inspiring 'New Wave' feel they owe to their essential Northernness – and to the sense of humour which is an integral part of the 'package'? We asked them.

Michael Parkinson

Nobody epitomizes more the sustained assault on the Southern-based middle-class stranglehold which gripped all aspects of creative life than Michael Parkinson. I remember cheering when, during his early 'Cinema' programmes, on television, he steadfastly refused to use a long 'a'. I had just been sacked from a new BBC Northern News programme for not having the necessary polish, so I particularly appreciated his stand.

Nobody could be more successful or good at his job than Mike and yet the road to the top has been Barnsley working-class, the local school and provincial journalism – Oxbridge, your days are numbered! He's a man who has absolute faith in his heritage and culture: how does he analyze its uniqueness?

Words are Michael Parkinson's business, first as a very fine journalist and in recent years as a highly successful television chat-show presenter, so it is not surprising that he considers that humour is a lot to do with speech. Even in the case of his favourite comedians, who are mainly from the North Country, he thinks that it is only partly true that they are funny because, where they came from – the depressed working classes of northern England – if you were not funny you went under. 'That's a bit of a cliché. There's an underlying truth to that, but I do not think it's the entire answer. Humour is a lot to do with speech. That sounds self-evident, but what I mean is *idiom*. I think that what makes the North-Country comedian *funnier* than his Southern counterpart is to do at times with accent and at times with cadence, with manner of speech. It is right the way through Northern society, too.

'When I was a kid I used to go to Barnsley Football Club, which in itself is a humorous experience. Every week in the terraces I used to stand next to a man whom my father called "Wobbly Gob". He had a great big mouth like Mick Jagger and he was an extraordinary improviser with words. I presume that he was semi-literate at best, but he had an extraordinary poetic way with words. He used to invent phrases, funny ones too, which were purely North Country and funny just in the manner of their saying, their delivery.

'I remember one occasion – and I later used this incident in an article – when he came out with something brilliant. Barnsley, who were in the second division in those days, had a winger called Johnny Kelly, a bandy-legged, bald-headed little fellow, and a genius. On this occasion they were playing Southampton, whose right full-back was the new star of British football, Alf Ramsay, later *Sir* Alf Ramsay. He was a very very immaculate player, never a Brylcreamed hair of his head out of place, his boots always shining with dubbin, and his shorts immaculate. The day that Johnny Kelly played him he had just been capped for England, and Johnny had the kind of day that every defender has nightmares about. He beat Ramsay inside out and turned him upside down. It was a total humiliation for Ramsay. Old Wobbly Gob was next to us when Ramsay's final humiliation came: Kelly struck the ball between Ramsay's legs and Ramsay fell down in the mud and sat there. And this man next to us shouted out. "Ramsay," he said, "Ramsay, tha's as much use as a chocolate teapot.'''

Mike sat talking in his house on the Thames near Maidenhead, staring across the sun-lit, tree-edged river for several seconds, contemplating the sheer perfection of that taunt hurled from Barnsley Football Club's cold terraces years before.

'Now, that is . . . As a writer myself, I'd give five years' salary to have invented that phrase. And it came from a semi-literate man who did not know what he was saying. In all the working-men's clubs in the area where I was brought up – a mining area in South Yorkshire – you would find people who had the same extraordinary way with words. I remember my grandfather – and he never used to say anything, my grandad – saying one day when we were sitting looking at the fire – they used always to have huge fires in those houses because, all being miners, they got their coal free – ''Ah'll tell thee what, our Michael, poke yon fire, it's sulking.'' Sulking . . . what an expression for a fire, but that's what it was doing. It wasn't glowing, it was sulking .. .

'There's a lot in the choice of words like that. It is apparent in Les Dawson's humour, in his way with words. I mean, when he describes his mother-in-law as having a face like a battle with spanners, that is purely and absolutely North-Country.

'Another thing about North-Country humour is the cruelty, the exaggerated cruelty, of it – when Les talks about his mother-in-law: jack-boot rash all over her body, that sort of thing. It is a great tradition of North-Country comedians who, in a very charming way – no, charming's not the word; they are not charming – benign way, almost, are saying the cruellest things.

'The one thing all North-Country comedians have in common is a pleasant visage. Think of Jimmy Tarbuck, think of Les Dawson, think of Eric Morcambe, think, going back, of dear old Jimmy James, and people like that. They all look pleasant, if not slightly gormless. And part of their humour is the deception they have – they say these extraordinary, cruel things, with this marvellous avuncular, benign face.

'Jimmy James was the classic example of that. Here was the guy who sold the Southerner every idea, every misconception he had of a North Countryman, and he came on looking slightly gormless. He pretended to be pissed all the time, he smoked incessantly – Woodbines – and he had this friend called Our Eli who was a real dope.

'There is one lovely piece from Jimmy James's act which has always seemed to me to be pure North Country. In other words, if you had translated it to any different accent, any different idiom, it would not have worked. In it, Our Eli comes on. He's got an old raincoat on, there's a huge rocket strapped on top of his head, and on his back he's got a vast parachute. Jimmy

James does the doesn't-really-see-him bit, puffs on his cigarette, looks him up and down. Eli says, "What do I do with this?" "You are going to be the first Yorkshireman ever to get to the moon," answers Jimmy. "How does it work?" asks Eli. "I light the blue touch paper," says Jimmy, "and you go up there at 7,000 miles an hour, you get on the moon and then you come back." "How do I do that?" "Well," Jimmy says, "what you do is you put your rocket on and come back to earth."'

It is clear that this act, plus Michael's loving re-creation of it, could go on for some time, so he shortens it a bit, and comes back to earth, where Jimmy James tells Eli that when he gets about 10 feet from the ground he pulls the rip-cord and the parachute opens. '"The parachute opens?" asks Eli. "Yes, 10 feet from the earth." And Our Eli says, "Well, what happens if it doesn't?" "Well, you could jump 10 feet couldn't you?" That is so cruel, and it's so North-Country.

'There is very little of Jimmy James on film, and it's a pity. He's my favourite comedian, and it's amazing how much many present-day comedians owe to him. There is a story Les Dawson tells which is similar in style. It is about two fellows with a greyhound.

'They get the greyhound to its first race, which it loses by about 5 miles. Couldn't do a bloody thing, this dog. So they have a meeting one day and one of the fellows says to the other, "That bloody dog – hasn't won a race yet." And the second fellow says they should get rid of it. "So, what should we do?" "Let's go down to the river and chuck it in." And the first fellow says, "I've got a better idea. Let's go to a field, leave it there and run away from it."'

The very funny, very graphic joke has Michael hooting with laughter. Our talk has become something of a wallow in nostalgia: he admits his work keeps him too much away from his North-Country beginnings, and he regrets it. 'They are natural comedians up there. I've played sport all over Britain, and – I'm not being biased about it, it's absolutely true – the funniest crowds are up in the North. They have an extraordinary wit.

'Here is a very typical Yorkshire joke. I was playing cricket for Barnsley one day with a guy called Ernie Steel. And Ernest had a habit of patting the wicket after every ball. He used to give it a right bloody thump with the back of his bat. On this day, the more Barnsley were in trouble, the more nervous he became and the more he banged the wicket. This went on for about ten overs, and one man in the crowd couldn't stand it any longer. As Ernest was in the middle of bashing the wicket, he shouted, "Eh-up, Steelie, tha ought to be careful. There's men working under there." And you have this picture of a great tunnel, 3,000 feet underground, caving in because of the bashing on top.'

One of the things a writer has to do if he is writing about the North Country, particularly North-Country humour, is to go back and refresh himself in the idiom, on the music of the language, because it is easy to get it wrong. It is often a key word that makes the difference between its being funny and unfunny. 'My problem is I don't get so many chances to go back any more and I am a bit out of touch. You do forget; there are little things they do, little mannerisms that make the thing unique. It is the alteration of the structure of the sentence, or the insertion of a word – a tribal word, I suppose you would say – and nobody else knows about it. "Eh-up" is a lovely word. Where did it come from? Eh-up? I know what it means – it means "hello" – but eh-up? It's a lovely daft word. Add "eh-up" to a story and its funny. Got to be.

'The mining community I come from is probably the funniest body of men I've ever come across. And very, very unique humour – absolutely deadpan. They never cracked, but by Christ, they were funny, they really were, *and* they knew they were; they knew exactly what they were doing.

'I had a Northerner friend called Bob Bradbury come down here a few years ago. He was a friend of my father, must have been about seventy-five, a beautifully dry humorist, and a great beer drinker. Beer down here, now, is one of the great North-versus-South points. According to Northerners, one of the reasons why Southerners are soft in the head is because they sup this bloody ale, and it goes straight to the frontal lobes and destroys them. Anyway, I took Bob to the Hind's Head (a very posh pub in Bray) and said, "What are you having?" and he said, "A pint." The pint came, and I knew what was going to happen, but I could not stop it at all. Bob picked up the pint – it was a Sunday morning, and the bar was crowded – and he looked at it and he said, "Eh-up, what's tha call this?" And the landlord – he's a very posh bloke at the Hind's Head – said, "Well, it's what you asked for: a pint of bitter." "Eh, we drown puppies in that stuff up in Yorkshire," said Bob, and he was right: there was no head on it, and it wasn't what he was used to at home.

'It is a very pleasant way of life down here, but what you do miss is that tribal kind of feeling there is up there. Down here it is such a mixture of people from all over England, it is difficult to find a real Southerner. Because of the massive influx of foreign tribes, the native tribes down here are swamped. Up there it is still identifiably a place, and they are very particular about who they let in and who they don't.

'I remember my father came home from work at the pit one day and said, "We've had a writer up at Grimethorpe, an American, and I've been showing him around." "Really," I said, "What's his name?" "Clancy Sigal." Well, he went on to write this book *They came from Dimlock*, which was hailed by the critics who knew nothing about it whatsoever as the best book about the mines since Orwell's essay. I read the book, and it was a load of crap, because what Sigal and his publishers had not realized is that up North they will let anyone in so far, and no further. They would never be inhospitable, and they would not be impolite to him, but they would tell him all the lies and never let him into what it was really like. They will give you cover-ups, you see, and tell a lot of baloney about the place, they really will. The truth is more difficult to get at and more interesting. It's almost a brotherhood. They can hate each other, but if any one of them is weakened, then the rest will move in around him.

'Bob Bradbury told me a marvellous story. He came down here at the time of the big strike when Heath took on the miners, and we were talking about it. "You know," he said, "it is bloody remarkable, in our village. We've been on strike for eight weeks and the bloody working-men's club's been taking three times more money during the strike than before." And I said, "But they can't be paying over the counter." "Not bloody likely they are paying for it. They are chalking it up. All the shops in the village are doing that – they're chalking it up – all except one, Baily's. She won't give credit." "What's happened to her?" "Oh, she's left the village." Mafia!'

Mike Harding

I was accosted in the cocktail bar of the Midland Hotel, Manchester. It was the head waiter of the hotel's famous French restaurant – I've known him for years – enquiring if I would be joining them for lunch. Knowing their pretensions, I reminded him that I was not wearing a tie. 'No matter *Monsieur*, we will provide you with one.' 'And the friend I'm expecting?' '*Oui, Monsieur*' 'Mr Mike Harding?' The waiter looked at me, then threw up his hands in that well-known Gallic gesture of hopelessness. '*C'est impossible!*' he cried and exited hurriedly, stage right.

For Mike is a raw little embarrassment running around Manchester – an extremely popular and successful television comedian who makes absolutely no concessions to those who, unlike him, set artificial standards which are both class-ridden and totally unnecessary. He loves and champions the people he was born and brought up with, he sees no reason either to move from the North or to flee from its values. We sat and talked over a modest meal in a typical Manchester cafe – served by a motherly waitress in black dress and white pinny. What he had to say was, to me, hilarious, illuminating . . . and very reassuring.

Mike began by putting the London theatre critics in their place. 'I've worked in London for the past five years, going down there, trying to build up an act and a following, and it's got bigger and bigger each time. I've found myself working with audiences with no trouble at all. Then you get the critics coming in – the critics who read Harold Hobson and Ken Tynan years ago, thought that this was the last word in theatrical criticism, and therefore judge everything from a city point of view. Any fellow who comes into it has got to be parochial: if his stuff comes from outside London or New York, it's got to be parochial. They can look down on you with a very critical and condescending eye. They did it to me a lot when I first went down there: "this *Northern* comic". It was sort of disparaging, as if "Northern comic" was some sort of stigma you carried round with you like a hump back, or one ear much bigger than the other. I know they will do it too with my next play that goes down there. I know the play works because I know where it *has* worked. But you can't beat the syndrome down there in London.'

Mike is sure if he had been born 'down there' in the suburbs he would not have been a comedian. If born a Cockney, he might have been, but: 'I don't think that places like Surbiton or Chelmsford produce people who have got big enough souls to take suffering and turn it into comedy. There isn't a great amount of suffering in Chelmsford, anyway – unless the dog from next door has come and crapped on your path. They tend to live a very mediocre life – all school fees and whether they can afford a holiday this year or not, or whether they should take the time at home so that Junior can get his 'O' levels.

For Northerners, or at least the Northern working class, there is not a lot of point in going and knocking someone for the way he lives, because he can't help it. Up there, they are victims, and as victims the only thing they can do is laugh at a situation.

'So many comics have said that humour has come out of adversity that it's a bit trite for me to repeat it – though it's true. I've known guys telling you about the First World War, and you've got to force them to remember the bad times. They come out with all sorts of things, like "Then there was the day the shelter fell in on Jimmy and we had to dig him out and he came out covered in crabs."

'The North has, on balance, produced the majority of comedians in this country, and some of the greatest as well – including Scotland, with people like Will Fife. The tradition has died out a bit now. The old working-class cloth-cap comic who was definitely recognized as an oily-handed son of toil, and who used to stand on the stage in gear very much like working gear for a night out on the town – he's mostly disappeared. After him you got the lounge-suited toreadors, and I worked for them; that was my baptism of fire, working the clubs around here when I was about sixteen or seventeen. In the rock and roll bands, playing to the audiences in those early days in the Manchester clubs, and following the stripper with the snake and the Chinese strongman act who tore a telephone directory with his teeth and had blokes on either side of him with a rope round his neck trying to strangle him, while he would grit his teeth and they would never be able to. You would get the comics coming on there, and there were some brilliant comics in this town then. There was a guy called Eddie Grunt – looked a bit like Fyfe Robertson, the old feller from the BBC news programmes – and he used to come on and do this aggressive sort of script, ad-libbing all the time.

'Then you got more into the lounge-suit sort of thing – a comedian was not a comedian unless he had a velvet bow-tie and ruffles all down the front. They were virtually telling gags; they were gag fellers rather than real comedians who could go on and talk about themselves within the class situation, within the geographical situation, talk about the town and the people and get humour out of that. To me, that is an act of creation rather than an act of repetition, which is all that the gag men do.

'The only older type of working-class comedians I can think of who are still carrying on are Wandering Walter, an eccentric comedian from round Preston way, who's still doing the act he did when he came back from the war in 1946, and Bobby Thompson, the Little Geordie. Now, Bobby's unintelligible to anyone from outside Newcastle or anybody who doesn't know a Geordie accent. He's bloody funny; there's the one about the wife packing up when they are going over to Blackpool and he says, "Oh, don't forget to pack the Oxo," and she's cutting it into slices for the week. Or there's the lovely one he does about being invited to London by the Queen. And he goes down, and: "Well, how's it going Lizzie, like? How's the corgies, how's the leeks . . .?" "Oh, they're canny, Bobby lad, canny. Would you like a cup of tea and something to eat while you're here? Bit of cake with your tea?" "Oh, that'll be lovely, like." "A meringue?" "Oh, no, you're not wrang – I like cake."

'In my work, I draw on my own background and my own experiences. I won't say my attitude is fixed because everyone is capable of redemption, but basically my comic album of life was welded and moulded in the streets of north Manchester, back of the ICI dye factory, the asbestos works and the cream-cracker factory. Eighteen years or so of your life in that situation – those are your roots. Consequently, even when I go down South or when I go to Australia, for instance, I am still very much the ex-patriate Northerner down under, doing the whole thing about Australian alcohol, the Australian language, and so on.

'The difference between North and South? There's a "Jack the Lad" attitude in the South. The Northerner's attitude is: "You can laugh at us, but while you're laughing, you don't know what we're up to behind your back." It's like Northern expressions. You find that they are always very direct, but said in a tongue-in-the-cheek kind of way. Things like: "The higher a monkey climbs, the more it shows its arse." That's a lovely saying – one of my grandmother's. She had another: "Street angel, house devil."

Some people sit back in a conversation in the North, and they let somebody rabbit on and get right out of order, really out, then they'll say things like: "If you had any more mouth, you'd have no face to wash," or "I'll bet your teeth are glad when you are asleep." They'll wait until the right moment, then they'll go straight in, and no one's left in any doubt about who's won.

'One thing Northern audiences don't like is for you to introduce ideas they can't handle. I used to do a piece about sex. I would start on about sex education in schools, and I'd say, "Isn't it funny: if a bloke plays around, puts himself about, he's a Jack of Lads. If a woman does it, she's a scrubber." With certain audiences, I'd get a laugh of recognition, as if they'd suddenly got it – no one had ever pointed this out to them before. I did it in Rotherham, and there was just an amazed silence, as if I was stating a fact.

'I don't want to make too much of the class thing. I mean, there are many different sorts of humour. There's the university humour of "Python" and "Beyond the Fringe"; there's the mad humour of the Goons and "Not the Nine O'Clock News"; and there's another sort of humour which I call relational humour. In America, Woody Allen can stand on a stage for half an hour just talking about his neuroses – relating stories about them. There are very few people in this country who have ever done that, very few people who are relational, who will stand up and relate rather than tell gags. In the past few years it has actually happened that people like me and Billy Connolly have done a combination of the relational approach, talking about what screwed up sorts of people we are as human beings. It is an almost dramatic-monologue style.

'One thing about working-class humour: it is never revolutionary. Never. It was always a way of taking the sting out of the boot heel that was on your neck. Like all those anti-foreman gags – for instance, there's a famous one about Khruschev visiting Mather and Platts. He's going round, and there's people turning in at half-eight instead of eight o'clock. And he says, "What time you start?" And they say, "Eight." "But they are coming in at 8.30." "Yeah," says the foreman, "and they have three-quarters of an hour tea break and an hour and a half dinner break and at the end of the day they are all pissing off at half-four instead of five o'clock." And Khruschev says, "In Russia, we never allow this because they come at eight and they work for ten hours." And the foreman says, "Ah, they wouldn't do that here – they're all commies, the bloody Northerners." You'll find the revolutionaries tend to be pretty boring, small-minded people anyway. No humour!

'When I started out, there were certain things I was told I could never say on stage – could never talk about farting, for instance. Farting – everybody does it! Obviously, you can get the laughter of recognition when you say things like: "The people who do it in lifts – they're the ones I want to get hold of, because there is nothing more anti-social than being stuck for seven floors in a lift cage where somebody's dropped one and then got out and you all get in and you've got seven floors with everybody looking at each other and nobody owning up and everybody looking at the ceiling – *everyone's* looking at the ceiling – and everybody's dying to say, "Oh, fuck! Who was that?" And yet nobody will do it. And the way they blame dogs – they'll kick the dog and say, "Get on, Rover, get on." It all makes a good story. Plenty of audience response. Here's another old Northern expression: "You can tell when the honeymoon's over when the groom farts in bed, shouts 'Burglars!' and the wife hides under the covers."'

We had a good laugh among the coffee cups over that one before Mike got serious again.

'My basic roots of comedy go back to radio, and the biggest single influence on me was radio comedians. Whenever I do a Northern mother-in-law, working-class, it's usually like Norman Evans's. I use the radio comedians' monologue style because it is very visual. Like the story of the bloke at a posh party who thinks the caviar is ball-bearings, the anchovies – well, somebody's made them by putting a sardine through a pencil sharpener. They're great, those pictures. I love doing it; I love getting a long story going and getting them with you all the way.

'The trouble with a lot of comedians up here, they went to London. At least, they got Londonized and imagined that London is the centre of everything. London is where all the

Arab sheiks come in and buy everything up. London is bullshit city. I've always regarded it as such and I always will regard it as such. It's where the merchant bankers are, it is where the money is shifted about and manipulated. The North is where the wealth is created and the South has always been the place where it is manipulated, gets spent.'

Mike feels very strongly about the way the old North has been knocked about, and his feelings are put to good use in his work. 'In Lancashire, there are many new towns. They've taken acres and acres of beautiful Lancashire countryside and destroyed it; left the city centres ghost areas. I'm a mad conservationist. I believe they have knocked down some of the most beautiful buildings in England in this city. OK, they were Victorian, and monuments to the Empire, but still they gave this area the character it had. I remember going through Burnley on my bike in Wakes Week, and thinking I had gone deaf. I'd never heard anything like it – the silence in the centre of that town was unbelievable. And then you look at it now, and other towns: the cotton industry is dead, had it, finished.

'You get London town planners who don't know Manchester, don't know what the city is about, and they come up and redevelop the city centre and rebuild it. I do whole acts round this theme and it goes well wherever I go, not just in Manchester. I might say something like: "You know how they get these Arndale Centres, don't you? They get these town councillors and, before they elect them, they make them sign a piece of paper saying that after they are elected to the council they agree to have their brains removed surgically. So they get a ferret and they make a small hole at the base of the skull with this ferret, and they pull the brains out with a bike pump, then they get them all in the town hall. The ring leader in the front, who has been programmed, says [and the Harding Manchester accent gets broader, more cotton-mill boss], 'Now we have been elected, what shall we do?' And someone at the back who has also been primed says, 'I know, let's knock bloody town down.' And another sixty-four councillors who just happen to be builders put their hands up and say, 'What a smart idea.' So they get a deaf, dumb and blind town planner up from London, who's later savaged to death by his guide dog so they can't blame anybody . . ." I go on about people being lost in there, and there's so many people with balls of string tied to bus stops outside that it's like a spider's web, and bodies lying down all over the place . . . This whole bizarre thing gets going about these Arndale Centres and mazes and everything, and you get laugh after laugh after laugh because people know what you are talking about, they recognize it all.'

Mike talked at some length about Lenny Bruce, the American anti-establishment comedian, and I asked him if he ever goes against the establishment in the way Lenny Bruce used to do. 'Yes, I do, but in a roundabout kind of way. I'm very anti-royalist. On my last tour, I would say I was overjoyed while in Australia to hear about Prince Charles: "The news came over, and I heard it on the radio. I was so overjoyed, I was so excited I had to get up and boil an egg. I imagined you all rolling about in the streets, rolling about with your legs in the air, delirious at the thought of spending £12 million. It's worth it," I said, "look at all the tourists you are going to get – £2 for a coke at Hyde Park Corner. Remember the lads who'll be making a butty or two down there! It's marvellous, wonderful news, give the old folk something to do, sitting all day in front of the telly. But I can't help wondering how he's going to manage, Prince Charles. He's a nice lad, but I can't help wondering how he's going to manage. To be honest. Think about it . . . he falls off horses, doesn't he . . .?" Gets a tremendous laugh!

'I've nothing against royalty, nothing against Margaret Thatcher. I don't think anyone ever does have anything against Margaret Thatcher, not even Dennis. You can just imagine it, can't you, them two getting ready for bed and she says, "Dennis, put that silly thing back in your pyjamas and get back into bed." I say, "She's used to looking down on the unemployed." Always gets a laugh, even in Tory strongholds – Croydon, I did it, Oxford: "You can't do that to me, Dennis, I'm doing it to the country."

'Mind you, you can't push things down people's throats. That's not what you are there for. You are paid to be an entertainer and give people a laugh. What you try to do is leave a little crumb sticking to their palate which they have to work out on the way home. You don't want to alienate your audience. You want to be loved. There is only so far you can push people without them closing their minds. The men in working-class audiences would go barmy if you said "fuck" in front of their wives, for instance.

'A lot of comedy is timing – I've seen people with good timing get a great laugh out of something that is rubbish, and I've seen people kill brilliant gags with bad timing. For example, there's a really old gag about a couple up against the back entry wall and he's giving her one, right? So he's giving her one and she starts nodding. And he says, "What's up?" and she says, "You've got me vest caught." I watched a comedian go on night after night before five hundred people, and he did not get a bloody spark with that joke because his timing was all wrong. There's got to be that little breath, that pause, that gets them thinking, "What's he going to say next, what's he going to say?"

'The other thing Northerners can do which Southerners can't is insulting humour: "Did you borrow that cup from next door, then?" or "Go next door and borrow a cup, we've someone posh coming for tea." When you've got nowt, there's no pretensions.

'There's a famous old joke about Oswaldtwistle. A Southerner, a rep with bags of samples in the back, asks, "Excuse me, I'm lost. Can you tell me where I am?" "Aye, Oswaldtwistle." "Er, how do you spell that?" "Tha doesn't spell it, lad, tha says it."'

The theme of Mike's play *Fur Coat and No Knickers* is pretensions – it concerns people who are all outward show and no inner substance. It is about two fellers who come out of the war with their gratuities. One starts a used-car lot on a bomb site and does very well – Mason, Tory councillor, the lot. The other doesn't, staying all his working life on the factory floor. The grandfather of the unsuccessful family is the play's *agent provocateur*.

One of the play's big scenes is the feast after the wedding of the working-class daughter to the Tory son (he whose mother Muriel was, according to grandfather, known in the war as 'Pearl Harbor' because she did more to knacker the Yanks than the Japanese). Let Mike take up the story: 'At the wedding feast, they start talking about royalty. The firebrand of a son of the working-class family works for the local alternative press, the *Grimesdale Alternative Press, Clarion and Bugle*. He's saying, "Bloody royalty, bloody this, bloody that." There's this big row about royalty, then it all goes quiet and everybody's very embarrassed and then, in the sudden silence, there's grandfather eating his food. He's got his flat cap on – morning suit and flat hat. He says, "Ah met Prince Philip once. He cum to open some new showers at Grimey Pit when ah were working there. Aye, he cum oop and spoke to me." "What did he say?" "He asked me how I liked the new showers." "Oh, that was nice of him. What did you say?" "Ah said, very nice thank you, but ah told him ah still couldn't get coal dust out of me balls."'

Mike is very much aware of the importance to a comedian of not leaving his environment, his class. 'I still live in the same area I was brought up in, still have the same sort of mates, though success does make you something of an outsider. They all like what I've got – after all, why do they all want to win the pools? But if you can get out of the two-up, two-down, outside-toilet-and-cockroaches and still stay in contact, that's good. My touchstone for reality is these streets here. I could never get big-headed. To me, I'll always be me.

'I'll go out regularly and just walk, just walk round the streets, watching it and smelling it. Even though they have just about virtually destroyed it, it still smells like my town. The people are still my people and I am still deeply involved in their situation and what happens to them.'

Mike emphatically rejects any suggestion that he might be a 'spokesman' for these people, but he is certainly doing his best to keep their traditions alive. He has a magnificent repertoire of old stories, funny, sad, bawdy and downright indecent, about every kind of Northern working man and woman, many of which he could never tell 'down there' because they would not be understood: tacklers' tales, for instance. A tackler was the man who came to feckle your loom, to set it up for weaving the different cloths, and he would fix it if it broke down. Tacklers were always disliked by the weavers. 'There are loads of tales about them, all to their disadvantage. There's the one about the tackler whose wife asked him to saw a foot off the yard prop, so he goes up to the bedroom and leans out the window and saws a foot off the prop. Then there's the one about the tackler whose wife wanted to mangle the curtains, so he drags the mangle upstairs. And he wants to get a piano upstairs so he ties a cat to it. "I had to keep whipping it," he says. And there's one about two tacklers coming home late at night. And one said, "Oh, we'll never get home. We'll have to sleep out. We'll go over there and get some kip." So they both slept all night with their heads on bits of concrete piping. And when they woke up in the morning, one said, "Oh me bloody head's killing me. Me bloody head!" And the other said, "Mine's all reet, it's all reet." "How did you manage?" asked the first feller. "I stuffed my pipe with straw first."

'The other Northern thing which is very important is the ability to laugh at death. Jokes about death which would not fetch a light in the South of England get big laughs here. There's a lovely one: she's dying and she says, "Albert, you know I'm going?" And he says, "Aye." And she says, "I want you to sit next to our Florrie in the car." And he says, "But I've never spoken to your Florrie for twenty years, ever since she opened the loft door and let all me birds out." "Do me a favour," she says, "just for me – me last wish. Have her in the car with you – me own sister." And he says, "No, I've not spoken to her for twenty years, I'm not going to start now. We pass each other in the street without looking at each other; at corner shop – we won't speak." "Please, Albert, just for me." "All right, I'll have her in the car, but it will ruin the day for me."

'Here's another. There's a fellow sitting by his wife's bedside. And she says, "I'm not long, Harold, I'm not long." And he's got the candle by the bed. And he says, "Don't fret, Lizzie, don't fret." "No, I've not got long to go." "I'll tell you what," he says, "I'll just pop down to the Co-op before they shut (they kept long hours then) and get some ham for the funeral tea. There's some going cheap – it's only got a bit of green on it, not much, but I can always scrape it off." "Well, thee go and get it, if its cheap" – she's just about to pop her clogs, but she's still trying to get things cheap. So he says, "Well, I'll just go now." And he gets to the door, turns and says, "If you go while I'm out, snuff the candle." Save a bit.'

As I was getting myself together to catch the train back down there, Mike related a bawdy story of old Manchester. It's reet vulgar, so, reader, if you do not like that sort of thing, stop here.

'Wherever there are pits – and that means all Lancashire, Yorkshire, Cumbria and the North-East – there are mining stories. In Manchester there are a dozen pits within the city boundaries. This story is about Bradford Road. The colliers are coming home from Bradford Road pit near Bellvue. It's Friday night and they're getting together and putting half a crown each in a bucket. A young collier comes along, only been there a week, and asks, "What are ye doing?" "Well, we're going to Dirty Nellie's on the way home. She gives us all a gobble, like, on the way home for half a crown." "Oh. Well . . . I'm in. Here's half a crown." "Right, you are in." So they all go off, and there's Dirty Nellie, sitting on her back step . . . Afterwards, they are all going home, and this young fellow is walking home down the back entry, and he looks down and realizes he has only one part of his anatomy clean. They'd all just come from the pits; no pit baths in those days – they'd go back to the missus and have a bath in front of the fire. And the young man says, "What'll I do when I get undressed at home? There's only me dick clean." So an older man says, "Na, lad, tha wants to do what I do – bat it wi' thee cap."'

Roy Hattersley

As I said earlier, the Northern invasion was not only confined to show business and creative writing. Politics too felt a snipe of hot red blood in the form of many young, mostly Labour, MPs, fresh from the new mint built by post-war educational emancipation. Fellows like Joe Ashton, Arthur Scargill and Roy Hattersley are all voluble, erudite New-Wavers who found their natural arena in politics and industrial relations. Below I quote a couple of excerpts from his prophetically titled auto-biography, *Goodbye to Yorkshire*, in which Roy Hattersley reveals the special quality of his Northern childhood.

First, here is Roy describing the atmosphere of his childhood and his father's part in it with typical Northern wit and grit in the face of adversity:

> In my youth, I had only one unique attribute – the belief that there was something tender and romantic about Barnsley . . . It began in 1935 when my father, after three years of unemployment, became a clerk at the Barnsley Labour Exchange, dispensing the dole on behalf of the Public Assistance Committee . . . For six months he made the journey between Barnsley and Sheffield Wednesday on a bicycle with an oval front wheel. Every morning and every night he travelled twelve miles forward and about the same distance up and down. There was no money for a better bike or even for a new front wheel. In any case, working-class families living in South Yorkshire in the early thirties expected life to be a bumpy ride.

Roy was only an infant of two when his home team, Sheffield Wednesday, won the Cup in Silver Jubilee year, 1935, but already he was being given an insight into the important things of life:

> Strapped in my push chair, I enjoyed a less-than-perfect view of the triumphant homecoming. But of one thing I am certain. The victorious captain holding the Cup aloft for all but the smallest and most restricted spectator to see was Ron Starling. I know because we talked about it in his paper shop during the dismal football days of the 1950s. We bought our papers there to ensure that, during an adolescence in which I was denied no advantage, I should handle a *Manchester Guardian* handed to me by a man who had held the FA Cup.

And here is Roy describing how he went up in the world:

> For a man who spent his boyhood on Spion Kop, an invitation to sit in the Wednesday Directors' Box was like a Royal Command . . . We did not come straight from the

wet and weather-beaten terraces. On the day I tried to put my umbrella up behind Manchester United's goal my father and I agreed that he was too old and I was too decadent for the concrete steps. Indeed, the Mancunians whose view I obscured made much the same point, though in different language. So we bought tickets for the extremity of the old stand and squinted from our seats over the corner flag. But we were still unprepared for the padded seats and the heated footrests of the first four rows at the centre line . . . We gave up Nuttalls' Mintoes. We learned to stroll nonchalantly into the ground at five to three rather than rush at the turnstile at quarter past two. We sat prim and proper and boasted to each other that we had watched Wednesday from every part of the ground. But I never felt confident in the exalted company until the late sixties.

Finally, a tribute to the Northern holidaymaker who can get the most out of life, even in a wet East-Coast seaside resort.

Bridlington is not at its breezy best on rainy days. Even in the self-assured seventies, its streets still appear to be filled with families who cannot or dare not return to their digs before six o'clock. They huddle against trees and in shop doorways, crowd under awnings or simply walk about getting wet. Yet they appear to remain incredibly cheerful, indomitably enjoying their holiday, a standing reproof to tourists on the Côte d'Azure whose day is spoilt when the white wine is not chilled. Their habits and their humour spread for miles around. They enliven damp afternoons in Sowerby Park, when the ladies' orchestra has retired from the bandstand and the long-bows are too wet for amateur archers to hold. They stand at the pavement's edge and watch the shivering donkeys trotting home. They queue outside Flamborough lighthouse, waiting their turn to climb its interminable stairs, so that they can look out from the lamp platform and enjoy a visibility of virtually nil.

Rene's got double pneumonia, she went for the fortnight!

Julie Walters

Julie Walters has sort of crept up on us. I was first aware of her in a series of almost grotesquely accurate portrayals of the horny upper-working-class housewife in early plays, and she also appeared in Victoria Wood's early TV plays. Then suddenly she hit the West End. I remember her getting rave reviews in _Funny Peculiar_, a painfully humorous Northern farce by Mike Scott in which she again was a seen-to-be-liberated Northern wife who gave her husband a fellatio treat under the hospital bedclothes.

I talked to her about that – you bet I did – and her other enormous successes in _Educating Rita_ and _Having a Ball_. She's a Birmingham girl but she's cornered the market in Northern female sexually frustrated zanies. She's played Lancashire farce both at home and away, so she should have something to say about the differences. I found her as fresh, fascinating and funny as her stage portrayals – almost unnervingly so – and I spoke to her as a fellow actor who's faced some of the challenges and prejudices she is facing now. Here's what we said.

Colin: I saw you in *Funny Peculiar* and *Educating Rita*, both in London. Mike Harding's got a play, *One-Night Stand*, opening soon in London and he fully expects to be patronized, just as I expect my *Roll on Four O'Clock* to be patronized, by the critics – theatrical Mafia, I call them. Did you do the two plays I've seen in London in the North as well?

Julie: Not *Educating Rita*. I did *Funny Peculiar* and *Breeze-Block Park* at the Everyman in Liverpool.

Colin: Did you notice differences in the audiences?

Julie: That's difficult. They did laugh much more readily in Liverpool, and lines that never got laughs in London did so in Liverpool. It was partly the type of humour, though – more local references. But, too, I noticed a feeling here in London, a general feeling – looking back over the two plays – that London audiences seem to have been educated by the critics. It's what the critics say that seems important in London; plays can live or die by what the critics say. London audiences can't seem to enjoy theatre in the same abandoned sort of way as they can up North, either, or respond as readily.

Colin: People in the North are not so theatre-going as they are down here, but this may be a good thing. People respond in a more positive way because they haven't got preconceived ideas of what the theatre ought to be. They also seem much quicker on the uptake. There is a particular laugh in the play you are in now, *Having a Ball*, that I know got a response when it was up North. That's when he takes the final underpants down and reveals a little plaster where he's cut himself shaving the pubic hairs off. This got a terrific laugh, yet it hardly gets anything down here. How do you diagnose that? Up North they must be able to: (a) spot it, (b) in a matter of seconds realize what it means, and (c) laugh. And I don't think they realize that here. Perhaps if he stuck a piece of newspaper on instead of plaster . . . like I do if I cut myself shaving.

Julie: Oh, he's done that now – sticks a piece of the *Guardian* on it.

Colin: Perhaps in the South they have looked at it, assessed it and rejected it. Perhaps you have to play them differently in London?

Julie: I don't think so. When I did the two plays in Liverpool, and then in London, I was new to it and had only been working a bit, but I did not notice anything different about the way we did the plays. Now, I do find, when I go back – like when I went to Sheffield to do *Good Fun* – there's no pressure; the critics aren't important. People just go for a good time.

Colin: I'm amazed in London how infantile are the middle-class audiences that go to these so-called West End comedies – I walk out of them, and the rest of the audience are chortling away.

Julie: Maybe they are more prudish, like harmless things more.

Colin: They certainly don't like being unnerved. When we did *Say Goodnight to Grandma* at the St Martin's, which is a comedy but ends tragically with the destruction of all three characters on stage, we got tremendous reviews, but after about six weeks the houses started to fall. The management came to me and said, 'Could you change the ending, because people are going out worried.' And I said that that was exactly what I wanted them to go out like. To go and look at themselves and see if they were doing the damage that was done on stage that night. And the manager said, 'But I want them to go out and say, "You must go and see *Say Goodnight to Grandma* – it's wonderful." They can't say that to their friends as it is.' It has to be *Cynthia's 21st* all the time.

Julie: Take Liverpool. People up in Liverpool have an innate humour; the barrage of wit that comes from the audience is fantastic.

Colin: There's a hell of a lot of ethnic character gone into the building of the Liverpudlian – he's a bit of Irish, a bit of Lancashire, and there's a lot going for him. It's a sea port, too, so there's lots of colour – or there was before it began to die.

Julie: I can think of a lovely incident that happened to a friend of mine working in Liverpool. He was doing Alan Bleasdale's film *The Muscle Market*. At the end of it he had to jump on the top of a double-decker bus to get away from the police. They were going to use a stunt man, but he said, 'No, no. I can do that,' and they said, 'All right' and let him do it, but nobody thought to warn the police or anybody about what they would be doing. So he started jumping on the bus, and there was a squad car up the road. They saw this happening, so they pulled out in front of the bus, stopped it and said to the driver, 'Do you know you've got a man on top of your bus?' And the driver said, immediately, casual, 'Yeah – it's full inside.'

Colin: A Liverpool comedian I know told me of working in a working-men's club there. The act before him was a Scouse Chinese conjurer who did an act with pigeons he made disappear. He had a hat and he'd say, 'Now the plidgin, the plidgin on the hand, now the plidgin in the hat. I put the plidgin in the hat and I put the hat on the head. I take the hat off and where's the plidgin gone?' And a voice said, 'It's fluffed off.'

Julie: You don't get that instantaneous response down South, or even in Birmingham. People might tell jokes, but that's different, somehow.

Colin: Anyway, Birmingham is Midlands. It is all people brought in as part of the great car-making culture. They don't have that community spirit they have in the North. Why do you think they have this humour in the North?

Julie: Well . . . the first thing that struck me is that it is such a poor place, and such a violent place, too. But it is also really warm – its heart is on its sleeve. Everything is coloured by their humour. Maybe it's an escape, a way of coping with the environment.

Colin: I find that the Southerner, or at least the middle-class one, wants to be reassured, to be comforted that his world is all right. That's why Alan Ayckbourn does so well. He could screw them, really nail them to the wall, he's got the wit, the perception and the ability, but he never uses them. The Mike Scott play *Funny Peculiar* – how did they take the last scene, you going down on your husband?

Julie: Up North they loved it. In London they were silent some nights. In Liverpool they absolutely roared, openly.

Colin: The night I saw it in London, a woman behind me said, 'What on earth *is* she doing?' and everybody got more of a laugh out of that than out of the scene.

Julie: They didn't want to put it on with that ending in London.

Colin: That's amazing, because people say, don't they, that for all his humour, the Northerner is prudish when it comes to certain things – especially sex. They say you can't get away with it, especially when their wives are present, yet there must have been wives present when you did that scene.

Julie: Oh yes, they all absolutely loved it. At the Liverpool Everyman there was always a core of middle-class people, but there were many working-class people in the audiences too, because we used to go round the pubs and do shows and the people who saw us there would come to the Everyman. I don't know that we would have got away with that scene in a pub, though. Our reception in pubs depended on the pub and the landlord, but on the whole we used to get a good reception. I can't imagine ever doing anything like that here – maybe in the East End we might.

Colin: There are so many good things about Northern humour. I love Northern funeral jokes.

Julie: I've got one – a good one. This chap was ill and went to the doctor. The doctor said, 'Well, I can give you a week, a week to live.' The chap took it very well. He went home to the wife and said, 'It's pretty serious. I've got a week, a week to live.' And the wife pulls herself together and says, "Right, you've got a week to live, you've got to enjoy yourself and we've got to face this together. So, right, what do you want to do?' 'Well, I'll tell you what I'd really like over the last few days. I'd like some really expensive food. That's what I'd like. I've never really done that.' 'Why not?' she says, and she's getting in *pâté de fois gras*, caviar, smoked salmon and all that sort of thing. Inevitably, of course, he gets terrific diarrhoea and says, 'Oh no, I'll have to stop this. Let's get back to all the old food. What have you got in?' 'Well, I don't know. You'll have to have a look in the fridge.' So he looks in the fridge and says, 'Ooh. There's some lovely ham here. I'll have some of that.' 'No you can't. I'm keeping that for the funeral.'

Victoria Wood

You know you're getting old when you see someone treading in your footsteps. It's even more unnerving if they step more nimbly and with more purpose than you did yourself. When I look at the career of Victoria Wood – writing as she does about the incidental dramas of simple living, and lighting up the screen with her painfully funny observations – I remember climbing up the same rungs myself and wish I could look with such fresh eyes *now* at what to others looks humdrum and inconsequential. The first play I wrote was about a rugby club tour. A pal of mine said, 'You didn't write that, you remembered it!'

Victoria Wood knows what to remember and how to build on it. She recreates for us the aspirations and pretensions of being young and foolish in the world of plastic discos and concrete hotels which is the Swinging North today. Unlike me, she remains part of it, living in Morecambe. Here she talks about her reasons for ignoring the call of the South.

There is no reason why Victoria Wood shouldn't live in Morecambe, of course. After all, Sadie Bartholomew thought well enough of the seaside town with the sunsets the guidebooks rave about to advise her son to change his name to Eric Morecambe as he was starting out on the road to fame and fortune. And Victoria Wood is also clearly marching along that same road: you don't get three Most Promising Playwright awards for one play nor are you described as 'the working girl's Joyce Grenfell' for nothing. So Morecambe it is, even though it is a long way from the nation's recognized centres of culture and showbiz razzamatazz. She is happy in her flat, a short walk from Morecambe's promenade, where she can write, compose songs and polish her stage act unhindered by stage or television people just dropping by.

Still in her mid-twenties, Victoria has already had several plays, which included her own music, performed on stage and television. *Talent*, a play with funny songs about a girl, Julie, accompanied by her fat friend, Maureen, trying to make it in showbiz in Lancashire was the one which took all the awards, including the *Evening Standard* award for Most Promising Playwright, made to its author in 1979. Last year she both wrote and acted in *Good Fun* at Sheffield's Crucible Theatre.

Victoria Wood has an ambition to be not a successful playwright but a successful stand-up comic. This is certainly in the Northern tradition, but hardly in the female one. There have not been too many successful women comics, but Victoria believes she can be one, in the all-singing, all-talking Joyce Grenfell style rather than in the monologue-with-stooge style of Hylda Baker.

At the outset she was a bit doubtful. She had won 'New Faces', the television search-for-a-star programme, in 1974, and decided to launch forth, inexperienced as she was. It was pretty disastrous, especially on tour as a support to Jasper Carrot, as she told David Robson of the *Sunday Times Magazine*, for one of their 'Lifespan' pieces: 'It was supposed to be my big break, but it was terrible. I died on my arse wherever we went and people just sat tapping their watches and thinking, 'Uuuhh . . . when's Jasper coming on?'

And, she told Robson, she's had the odd horrific evening where she has been booked for a student ball and sat captive behind a piano and a bank of gladioli trying to communicate with a mob of drunks who are falling about being sick and putting ice cubes down girls' frocks. 'I felt so embarrassed when the social secretary came up and gave me the money and said: "Of course, it's not your fault. You were terrific." And you know they don't mean it. And they grudgingly count out 150 quid and you think, "I haven't done anything to deserve this money." But you don't give it back.'

Victoria has developed a lot since those early days. Writing songs at a day's warning for Esther Rantzen's 'That's Life' programme, grabbing an hour's sleep, then rushing down to London to perform them helped a lot, and being on Radio 4's 'Start the Week' put her name and style before the listening public. So she began carving out a career for herself as a cabaret artist.

These days, she told David Robson, her best audiences are to be found in theatres and art centres – 'mainly young people or older people who think they are twenty-one but aren't!' But she hopes to get so good she can play to anybody, not just people to laugh at jokes about marijuana and pre-menstrual tension – or even cystitis: *Good Fun* is about the problems besetting an arts centre trying to arrange a social get-together for a group of sufferers from the problem. 'Is it possible?' she asked Robson. 'I think it's a bit possible. I don't think it's a lot possible, but I've got to believe it's possible otherwise I might as well shoot myself. I can't go on doing plays all the time – it will drive me up the wall.'

Her work is funny and more forceful, more abrasive now than it was. A lot of it, though by no means all, is about the problems of women, seen from the point of view of a woman, but she's not aggressively women's lib. She has come to realize that the problem for a female comic is the same as for a female bank manager or company director: you have to be more forceful and aggressive than comes naturally to most women because, if you are not, you won't be noticed or taken seriously.

But the subject matter does not have to be female-dominated. She believes in equality, of course, but does not see the need, or the desirability, for women writers to be labelled 'feminist'. In fact, like that other great Northern comic writer, Alan Ayckbourn of Scarborough-by-the-sea, Victoria Wood of Morecambe-by-the-sea writes about people she has seen and heard, doing things she has noticed with an eagle eye for detail, and worrying about all the problems of life which she knows about because she has worried about them too – even though, to middle-aged me, she's still a kid.

Alan Price

I'm not a jazz fiend, so the professional Alan Price is largely beyond my ken, but the private bloke – my fellow director at Fulham – I enjoy calling a friend. He's soccer and I'm Rugby League but we all have our problems and I don't hold it against him. He's a dynamic character, a quality which, even to my ignorant ears, emerges in his music. He's also flat, hard and practical under his buoyant exterior, in the true Northern tradition. He's been through it all, seen it all, been an international pop star since I was in 'Z-Cars', and that's centuries ago.

We were all part of the marvellous Northern sixties thing in those days. Alan enjoys reminiscing, talking about the good and the bad times . . . we talk the same language. He lives near me – our boys play together. Over a drink, here is what he had to say about the North and what it's meant to him to be Northern and to live with its sense of humour.

Alan Price was born and brought up in the working-class North-East. Today, he's well-known and well-off, lives in the South, and plays his golf on the carefully tended links of the very middle-class Richmond Golf Club. His North-Country background is still very much a part of his make-up, though, and he can look at his present position in the world with a certain cynical amusement. He was the first pop star ever to be elected to the Richmond Golf Club, where they have counted royalty among their members, and he's wryly amused at the fact that he is obviously the club's token North-Country working man – its spokesman for the working class, in fact.

Alan makes a joke of the occasion – it was during the usual Sunday afternoon session at the nineteenth – when he felt obliged to speak up for the ordinary working man during a rather hysterical discussion on the general wickedness, and all the rest, of strikers. His short speech was followed by a deadly hush before the conversation took up where it had left off. But now, when he goes in on a Sunday, there's one man who always greets him with an 'Eh-up, comrade' and a few bars of 'The Red Flag'.

He thinks that that dash of cynicism is a major part of Northern humour. Where he comes from — he was born in Jarrow and lived for a time in Newcastle — the arch comedian is Bobby Thompson. 'His humour is all based on the Andy Capp, Tarzan-and-Jane battle between the sexes. There's nothing so unequal as the distribution of household duties; for the man, it is work and nothing else, for the woman it is work all of the time and never getting paid for it. So there's the constant battle for the pay packet between them, and the constant battle between the man and his mother-in-law. The mother-in-law has got out from under, so she can inflict all the venom and all the frustrations from her own relationship on her daughter's, and thereby try to protect her.

'It was really a matriarchal society up there, despite Bobby Thompson. The women kept the thing ticking over, even when the men had no money. I've just been reading that in the working-men's clubs up there, the women are now trying to get equal rights, so the battle's still on.'

Another major thread running through North-Country humour, as Alan sees it, is its tendency to abstraction: it's about something you haven't got. He tells a story about the father of one of his friends which nicely illustrates both the cynicism and the abstraction. 'I went to see him in Nottingham once, round about 1966 or so, and the walls of his room were filled with the Left Book Club, *The Road to Wigan Pier*, Victor Gollancz, and what-have-you. He was one of those real working socialists. He said to me, "Let me tell you something. Before we had socialism, we thought there would be art for the people, there would be dancing round the maypole at the factory. We really thought it was going to be something. Before we had a socialist government, we had no money – couldn't booze or anything, so on a Saturday night we'd walk from Long Eaton into Nottingham town centre." There would be a great crowd, he'd walk up to it, and it was the butcher's, where everyone was watching the bacon slicer. It was one of those big slicers, with the handle

going round; it would slice the bacon, then come back
. . . and that was it. He'd walk back to Long Eaton, and that was
his night's entertainment. "Then," he said to me, "then we got
an effing socialist government, and now we can afford the effing
bus fare into Nottingham to see the bacon slicer." ' The story's
told with a roar of laughter. It is something to be proud of, not
depressed about.

And there is another funny story he tells with pride. This one
is about his mother, and it's about struggle and adversity, too.
The punch line's memorable.

Alan and his group, The Animals, had had months on the
road, travelling, living, sleeping and existing in a van as they
dashed the length and breadth of the country from one
one-night stand to another. 'We were at the Floral Hall in
Southport. Our first record had just taken off and we should
have been famous, but we didn't have two pennies to rub
together. I think I had 2s 11d in my pocket. We were all
exhausted. After the show, we tore off the stage and I was first
into the van. Then there was a hold-up – something had fallen
off the bottom of the van, and we had a row, and there was no
money for petrol to get us down to Southampton . . .

'Anyway, I decided I had had enough. I picked up my
suitcase and walked down that great long flight of steps they
have there. It was the dead of night, no one about, pitch black. I
sat in the town square, with the clock chiming out the quarters.
After an hour or so, I went back, but they'd gone. So I sat in the
town square some more, and a policeman came up: "What are
you doing?" "I'm going home?" I said. "Where's home?"
"Jarrow." "Jarrow?!" "Aye, I've just left the band, so I want to
get home, see." "Here, son, we'll take you to the outskirts of
Southport." So I got in the police car and they drove me to the
middle of nowhere and put me off. By this time it was pissing
down with rain, and I'm standing with my suitcase and I'm
exhausted. One o'clock, then two o'clock, then finally a lorry
came along and the guy driving was going all the way to
Middlesbrough and he let me in. He threw my case in and I
climbed up into the cab. It was so warm – it was fantastic. I slept
all the way to the A1 near Middlesbrough, where he dropped

me off. I got another lift from a guy who was on Benzedrine. He was driving a furniture truck and shaking . . . Anyway, he took me in and bought me breakfast, and got me to Newcastle. With the 2s 11d I got a bus to Jarrow. I got home, knocked on the door, my mother answered, and I said, "I've come home."

'And she looked at me – you know the way mothers look at you – and out came this classic line, "Well, as long as you know what you are doing."''

Sport

If you talk about the North you talk about sport, and talking sport is talking humour. The men who fought their way up through the ranks to become top-class sportsmen, especially in the old days, were essentially great characters. Maybe not all extrovert and voluble but they needed an extra ingredient in their make-up to help them rise above the hordes of talented young lads who were equal in their resolve to make it to the top. To my mind that ingredient was a complete confidence in themselves, who they were and what their abilities were. Confidence breeds humour. The man who is contained enough to lie back, observe and laugh has to be secure in the knowledge of his own special worth.

The North, with its great sporting traditions, has always produced such characters in abundance, both on and off the field, playing, administering and watching. A society built on basics has very little time for pretensions, relationships are invariably bluntly face to face, and with all social cosmetics removed the great Northern wisecrack flourishes. Humorous incidents abound at every level of Northern sport and, having a keen interest and involvement for as long as I can remember, I could reel off hundreds. At the risk of ruining every after-dinner speech I now make, I'll tell you a few.

Billy Bremner remembers playing for Leeds United at Elland Road against Manchester City. Halfway through the first half the ref injured himself and had to be helped off the field. As one of the linesmen took over, a plea came over the tannoy for anyone with FA credentials to make himself known. Immediately a cry arose from the crowd and out stepped a tubby little man, throwing off his overcoat like Superman to reveal a full referee's outfit underneath, complete with badges of qualification. He was given a flag and hared into position with a delighted cry to Bremner: 'We're all right now, Billy!' Franny Lee, playing striker for City, threw up his hands: 'Jesus,' he said, 'We've *no* bloody chance now!'

Rugby League, my game, has a fund of stories. One of my favourites is of the forward who was laid out cold. He came to surrounded by his team mates and receiving the cold sponge. His eyes widened in horror. 'I can't hear, I can't hear!' he cried. 'Course you bloody can't,' said his trainer, 'nobody's said owt yet.'

A famous Australian wicketkeeper once told me about playing against Yorkshire at Headingly. He was joined at the crease by the last man, with Australia needing two runs to take a first-innings lead. The crowd was enormous, the gates closed; people were sitting on roofs and hanging from trees. The tail-ender's first ball hit him fairly on the pads, patently missing leg stump. An enormous appeal went up from all around the ground – even the pigeons had a go. The umpire's finger went up and Australia were all out. As they were walking off, my friend said to the umpire, 'That was never out?' 'I know,' was the reply, 'but I'd rather please 30,000 Yorkshiremen than one bloody Australian!'

Imagery plays a large part in Northern humour. The ability to pick out exactly the right, often ludicrous, invariably earthy, simile is a hallmark of Northern wit. Whilst I was commentating once with Harry Rigby on Crown Green Bowls for television, one of the players had to leave the field. 'He's probably been caught short, Harry,' I said. 'Aye,' said Harry, 'it's a long way to the gents here and all, you need a bladder like the R101 to play bowls on *this* Green.'

The list of Northern characters in sport to whom we could have talked is endless – we've had to content ourselves with a cross section of the most colourful.

Lawrie McMenemy

Stepping out from the classy Royal Garden Hotel in Kensington one evening, my wife and I were accosted by a tall handsome devil with curly hair, broad shoulders, flashing eyes and an accent that made 'When the Boat Comes in' sound like a Nancy Mitford production. He bowed, the swine, took Pat's hand, kissed it and asked what she was doing with a fat, ugly bugger like me. I told him it was none of his business. It was Lawrie

McMenemy, the vagabond king of Southampton. He's not only a successful football manager, but also a raconteur and well-known teetotaller. His only blemishes are: (1) that he was once with the Brigade of Guards, and (2) that he turned down the job with Leeds United. Other than that he's completely unspoilt – mint condition.

What does he feel his Northernness has done for him, and still does on the warm, palmy South Coast? We spoke to him in his office at Southampton FC.

It is eight years now since Lawrie McMenemy left the North, via the North-East where he was born and such fortresses of Northern Football as Sheffield and Doncaster, to take up the managership of Southampton Football Club. His team is doing very nicely these days and Lawrie likes life in the South, but he still hankers after the North. To keep himself 'in touch' he plays tapes in his car, while driving to and from Vicarage Road, of the Geordie comic Wee Bobby Thompson, who must be just about incomprehensible to any Southerner.

Because he is a successful football manager and something of a personality in the game, and because he's a pretty good bloke anyway, Lawrie McMenemy is constantly being asked to speak at football functions, dinners, meetings and the like. He admits he's not a professional at the speech-making and joke-telling game, but over the years on the speech circuits, he's picked up some great stories and he's evolved a style which gets a good response from his audiences.

It was not always so. 'When I first came down here, the first function I ever went to was on the Isle of Wight. It was a supporters' group, and I went with one of my staff who was from Manchester. I was a bit nervous, because I was new to the place and they were all looking to see who I was and what I was going to do. I remember trying to trace my career, saying I had come down from the North Country, and when I was there I used to have to make long drives, over the Pennines, to glamorous places like Rochdale and Halifax and the like . . . not a flicker, not a smile.

'I realize now that they did not know what Rochdale and

Halifax are like because they never go anywhere up there, whereas Northerners are prepared to come down here and not be too worried at the idea. It would not even enter the minds of people from the Isle of Wight that they might go up there. They would not go to Blackpool from here. They have an image of Blackpool – I'll bet there are not many people from Hampshire have been to Blackpool.

'I remember at this Isle of Wight meeting trying to inject some humour into it. I said that I would go to places like Halifax and I would go into the football club, and not want to be noticed watching the opposition, would put down £1 and say, "Two, please," and the ticket seller would say, "What do you want, forwards or half-backs?" The game would have started, a big roar would go up, and I'd get up that big bank they have there and ask, "Have they scored?" and someone would reply, "No, the pies have arrived."

'There was no response to all this, not a bloody flicker. There was only one bloke laughing and that was the bloke from Manchester who had come with me. I know the jokes were old – most Northerners probably learned them in their nappies – but the thing was, that there was no flicker from the Southerners at all.

'I think I may have changed over the past eight years. I go right round the country now, and maybe I have mellowed, or the accent is not so hard, but I have some football stories now which go down well everywhere. I tell several, pointing out the difference between North and South.'

One of Lawrie's jokes is more like a short story, and it is told with an actor's sense of timing and delivery. 'In it there's a fellow going across the Tyne bridge one day. It's very early in the morning, and he's on early shift at the Central Station. Nice day – the one day in the year when the sun shines in Newcastle – and there's no one around, not a car, no traffic. The worker can just see ahead, about half-way along the bridge, a fellow just making to jump into the Tyne. (If you jump into the Tyne, you'll never come out, because it will kill you!) So the early-morning worker runs up to the fellow and says, "What the hell are you doing?" And the bloke says, "Leave us alone, I'm going to end it all. I'm finished. I've had enough." But the worker, pulling on his leg to hold him back, says, "Oh, but listen, you'll never wake up again in the mornings and hear all the birds twittering and whistling . . ." and the feller replies, "I hate bloody birds." "Oh, but listen," continues the worker, "you'll never be able to see all the little kids at school, skipping along, and hear their laughter ringing out . . ." "Children – I can't stand them." And he's just about to dive in when the worker thinks of something else. "Oh, but listen, you'll never ever be able to go back to St James's Park and see Jackie Milburne tearing down the right wing, dragging the ball back, beating three men and chipping into the far corner of the net!" And the feller says, "Who's Jackie Milburne?" "Get in, you bugger!"'

Lawrie tells this joke as a way of getting people to understand the passion felt about football in the North. He says that down in the South, where Southampton FC have been having a lot of success, the supporters come and sit as if they were at the pictures: it's not an important part of their life, football. 'It's not like a religion to them, it's not like missing Mass if you don't go, which it is in hot-bed areas. They are all in the North: no hot-beds in the South. There is no tradition, as in the North, where it goes back to the Depression. When there was no work, football was the release for the working man. Those areas where the Depression hit hardest – Liverpool, Merseyside, Manchester, the Black Country, Tyneside and Glasgow – they are hot-bed areas. All the other areas, like Ipswich, Norwich, Nottingham and Southampton, they've all had success in football, but it's been with people. Clough, Bond, Robson, McMenemy, whoever, you identify with people, because there's been no tradition. In the hot-bed areas, they are going to be successful whoever's manager or plays for them because the area demands it, and that is the difference.

'I often say, as an analogy, that down here if they want to go out and feed the seagulls, and the weather's cold, they'll put the bread down the toilet and flush it. And that's the difference. Max Boyce says he could tell that Tyne bridge story and insert Gareth Edwards instead of Jack Milburne, and his Welsh audiences would understand and appreciate the feeling behind it. The background is the same: pits and hard work.

'I like painting a picture of northern football for my audiences. I tell how when I was a kid I used to go to Newcastle. The gates would be closed, but you couldn't afford to get in anyway, so you waited till ten minutes from the end when they opened the gates. You used to nip in and they'd pass you down over their heads to the front – nowadays they'd let you drop, stand on you and kick your head, or something, but then they used to pass you over their heads and they would get you to the front and sit you on the wall. And that was great. It was magic just to sit there and watch those black and white shirts. Though, looking back, I must admit there was the odd bad game – even though you would never have admitted it then. I might say, for my Northern audiences, that it gets a bit nippy up there in Newcastle; I've got to admit it gets a bit cold, and some days you are standing on the Kop and you are hoping someone has a pee down your leg. Now, down South I'd get thrown out for saying that.

'Not long ago I was on a panel down here with Kevin Keegan, Dennis Law and Jack Charlton. There were 1,200 or 1,300 people there, mainly to see Keegan, and they hadn't asked Jackie Charlton a single question for about half an hour. He was getting a bit bored and looking at the ceiling when there came a question right from the back: what had he put in Terry Curran's tea? Terry Curran was a player who was here a couple of years ago and he was not good. I sold him to Jack Charlton and he scored a lot of goals in his first season with Jack. Mind, the fact that he was two divisions lower helped, but the fellow at the back didn't recognize that. So: "What have you put in Terry Curran's tea, Jack?" And Jack, in his straightforward Northern manner, in front of a crowd of women and kids and the rest, said, "It's not what I put in his tea, it's what I stuck up his arse." I just buried my head, like; that sort of thing I would never have told.

'But I do tell people about games when I was a kid standing on the Kop and the weather was so cold they had to chip the dogs off the trees. I build it up into a picture of a game that wasn't going too well, of a game so bad that the crowd was getting restless, while Lord Westwood, the famous director and Football League chairman who wears a patch over one eye and has at times been called a one-eyed bandit, moved his patch from one eye to the other. Two old-age pensioners got up on the running track and started to fight. In those days they did not have lots of coppers to separate the fighters, so they were getting stuck in. One copper 50 yards away was strolling down towards them, but in the meantime there were wallets and dentures and pension books flying around. Then eventually the copper came up. "Ah well, lads," he said, "what are you doing, diverting everybody's attention off the game?" And the young 'un, who was about eighty-seven, said, "Don't blame me, I've just caught him trying to get a season ticket into me pocket."

'I find that that sort of joke is purely Northern, and I could tell that without thinking up there, and they would react to it, whereas anywhere else, I would have to think twice. Unless it's in a hot-bed, and then it's a doddle.

'I like to talk about characters in the game – Stan Mortensen, for instance, a very funny man, a Geordie, who lives in Blackpool. Stan played in the 1953 Wembley Cup Final, which is now called after Stanley Matthews, who also played in it, even though it was Mortensen who scored three goals. I often tell the story about Stanley Mortensen and the voice in the crowd telling him whom to give the ball to. The story starts with Stan telling me, "Well, at least I thought that at Wembley I wouldn't hear that loud-mouthed bugger who is always having a go at me at Blackpool. This is it, I'm at Wembley, 100,000 people, the band's playing, the lot." Then, he says, "We'd just got started, I got the ball, and I was just going to deal with it, when I heard this bloody voice from the back at Wembley: 'Give the ball to Matthews.' So, I thought, 'Dear, oh dear, I can't even lose him here!' So I laid the ball off to Matthews. Next time I got it, the Voice cried, 'Give the ball to little Ernie Taylor.' So I knocked it off to him. The next time I got it there were three great 6-foot defenders right there, breathing down me neck. I could hardly see daylight. So I looked up at the stand, and the Voice said, 'Use your own discretion!'"

'Stan used to say that in the pit village where he came from they were all natural athletes. He says that he remembers in 1933 an uncle of his doing the 100 yards in 6.2 seconds and that was in his pit boots – he fell down the shaft.

'The trouble with the average football crowd today is that it's more blasphemous, more bad-language than witty. But I have heard some nice examples of the wit of the Northern football crowd. There was a good one in a game when a dog had run on, and they couldn't catch it, and a wit in the crowd shouted, "Leave the dog on and bring the centre forward off." There was another beautiful one last season at Liverpool. Crowd of 47,000, and Southampton playing very well, winning 1–0, which is against all the laws of gravity and everything else up there, winning well and deserving to, and the famous Kop were in full cry. Liverpool got the inevitable penalty, and the match was a draw, but in between times, a cat came on at the far side and started to make its way across the pitch. At the time it came on, the Kop were shouting, "Attack, attack, attack!" and I swear that in the middle of the shouting, as the cat appeared, the cry changed from "Attack, attack, attack" to "A cat, a cat, a cat!" A really good play on words, that.

'Fred Trueman is another great sporting character with many jokes told round his name. There must be enough of them to fill a large book. I've heard a good few of them, some of the best from Mick Cowan who played cricket with Fred for about nine years – he opened the bowling with him. Mick says that Fred was the one with the car – this was when they were young – and he had to pick up Cowan as he went through Doncaster. Mick used to stand on a corner waiting, and Fred was always about half an hour late, so when he did turn up, according to Mick, it was like the Royal Scot picking up a mail bag as he got in the car and was whipped through Donnie. The next thing would be the whine of the police siren, and up would come the cop, strolling forward, hitching his trousers up, looking in the car, then obviously showing recognition but pretending not to. "'Ullo, 'ullo, are you trying to drive as quickly as you bowl then?" Trueman, according to Cowan, would reply, "Don't be bloody silly, lad. If I did you wouldn't even see me, let alone catch me."

'Once into Headingley, everybody in the team would want to know how Fred was, and they could tell by certain signs. I can recognize this; the outside people see all the glamour of sport, but we live it, and it's not all that glamorous, because we live with each other for eleven and a half months of the year. But we do know our own song; my players know if I am bombing a bit and I know how they are. This is what it's about – psychology. So I can identify with Mick Cowan when he says the whole Yorkshire team would wonder how Fred was and if he had had a bad night. They could tell when he was chirpy. The two opening batsmen would come out, and the fielders would all be waiting there. Fred would let them get down the steps, then he would shout so that everyone could hear, "No need to shut the gate after you lads, you won't be that bloody long." And everyone would wink and nudge and say, "Good old Fred." He would wait till they got half-way to the wicket, then he'd shout up to the pavilion, "If there's any phone calls for these two, just tell them to hold on." All this is very intimidating to the young batsmen.

'Cowan's description of the opening ball of a Trueman over is epic. The whole ground would always stop for Trueman's first ball; they wouldn't sell score cards, the ice-cream men would stop and the whole ground was tense and waiting. Cowan used to field right in front of the bat, that silly position where if they hit you they really hit you, called short leg or something like that. As a result, he would be looking at the batsman and not seeing Trueman. And he would hear these size 10½s pounding in and pounding in. The batsman would start off with his eyes open and they'd get bigger and then they would narrow to a slit and then the colour would slowly drain from his cheeks down to his chin and then the boots would stop and there would be a blur and the next thing there would be a scream and the batsman would crumple up in a heap. A voice would come round from behind Cowan: "Always put the first one in their balls; it makes their eyes water."

'The trouble with Northern people in sport is that they are very insular and very blinkered. They don't recognize that there is anywhere else in England. Yorkshire won't even have anyone born outside Yorkshire play for them. The North-East football reporters, for instance, know everything about world football and they are the best, even though Newcastle is struggling to stay in the second division and Sunderland have just got back into the first and they all get lost if they go past Scotch Corner. They are very like the Welsh, who think they are the best singers in the world, but never stop singing long enough themselves to listen to anybody else.

'In the North-East they have their own brand of humour. I've got cassettes by two people called the Dixielanders at their club. They are a group, went round the working-men's clubs for about twenty-five years and then they got so wealthy they bought their own club. It's like an old-fashioned music hall – stage, tables and people sitting shoulder to shoulder, pints of beer, pease pudding and stoddie cake – and they book up for a year ahead. They've got two comedians, and musicians who come in and out. That's it in a nutshell. Their comedy is all about when they were kids and their listeners identify. They will talk about nit nurses, when the nurse came round at school with a great hard comb looking for nits in the kids' heads. Bath was on a Friday night and the Dixielanders will talk about that and have the audience roaring with laughter. The kids laugh, too; my kids laugh and they are not even true Geordies now, and they've certainly never known the nit nurses.

'And what about Bobby Thompson, whose record came out at the same time as 'Grease' and outsold it three times over. He's become a legend now at seventy-two. He's smoked Woodbines all his life, and no one would understand him if he came down here. Even I find it difficult to pick up on the cassette every word he says. But his humour is all about rent books and dole queues and 'The Dole is My Shepherd, I shall not Work.'

'I never had a nit nurse at school, and I was never really poor, though we were hard up, but I identify with everything he says and I cling on to that. Now, when I get into my big car and get home to my big house, that's what keeps me sane and normal – my memory of days like that. People like Bobby Thompson and the Dixielanders are exactly what Northern humour is about. They make a living of reminding people of their heritage.'

Bill Shankly

The late Bill Shankly was not a Northerner in *our* sense of the word. As a Scot he was even Northerner than Northerners, but he wasn't Northern English. He was Liverpudlian by adoption, and professed an undying love and admiration for the city and its people. He was a caustic wit in his own right, of course, and the corridors of sport echo with tales of his verbal exploits.

Bill, another teetotaller, had a great fondness for fine blended tea. When he was manager of Liverpool and they were due to play Manchester United, Bill rang up his friend, Matt Busby, *their* manager, to discuss the game. Matt's wife, Jean, confessed to Bill that Matt was unwell and feared that he would not be able to attend the match. This would be a great blow to United, of course, to be without their manager in such an important confrontation. Bill immediately said he would send round some herbal tea for Matt, an offer which Jean gratefully accepted. On the Saturday morning of the game Bill rang again. 'Thanks for the tea,' said Jean. 'Matt's taken some, but he doesn't seem any better.' 'Who said I wanted him *better*?' was Bill's reply.

He was a marvellous man, blunt, scrupulously honest, compassionate, a life-long socialist . . . and, come to think of it, he fits into the Northern mould very nicely.

My one memorable experience of true Scouse wit occurred when I was appearing at the Liverpool Playhouse. One of the cast had recently broken his arm. It was out of plaster but he'd been given a small rubber ball to squeeze, to strengthen his grip. Coming out of the stage door one evening, he dropped it, and had to chase it, bouncing, along the pavement. Two little boys watched him go by: 'What else d'yer get for Christmas?'

Bill was steeped in such stories, and the best tribute to his humour is to let it speak for itself.

Some of the things Bill said – the pithy comments that have become part of the Shankly legend – were said with a Scottish pawkishness that forty-five or so years of football with Northern English clubs did not manage to subdue.

There is, for instance, the story of Bill in Amsterdam with the team for an international. When he filled in the hotel registration form, he put 'football' in the 'occupation' slot and 'Anfield' in the address slot. The pretty receptionist objected: 'You have to write in where you *live*.' 'Lady,' said Bill, 'in Liverpool there's only one address that matters, and that's where I live.' Then there was the crack about Brian Clough he made to a sports journalist: 'He's worse than rain in Manchester. At least God stops the rain occasionally.' Again there's the epitaph on a player he once transferred from Liverpool. Asked why, he said, 'He's got the heart of a caraway seed.'

Bill retired as manager of Liverpool in 1974, and had no official role in the game after that. But until his death he was still one of the great men of football, someone whose friendship was claimed with pride, even by people like the taxidriver who drove us from Liverpool railway station to Bill's house, who may have met him only once or twice.

In the 1980–1 season, Bill chose to give some advice to non-League Altrincham who found themselves pitted against mighty Liverpool in the FA Cup, and the fact made the national newspapers and the main evening news on television. Was Shankly being a bit disloyal to his old club? Of course he wasn't. Maybe it was that pawkish Northern humour surfacing again, as he gave deadpan advice on how to deal with the Liverpool men, knowing full well that this would be no replay of the David and Goliath scenario – and it wasn't: Liverpool won handsomely.

Before his death in 1981, I was fortunate enough to have the opportunity of talking to Bill about the humorous side of football at his home near the Everton practice ground in Liverpool. (Another example of the Shankly humour?) It was easy to see that football was still the main interest in the life of a man who, when someone once asked him if he saw football as a matter of life or death, replied, 'A matter of life or death? Nay, it's more important than that!' Neat and trim as ever, Bill was wearing a red sweater carrying the Liverpool emblem. There were books, tapes and records about football, a heap of fan mail waiting to be answered and, in a corner, a huge, elegantly mounted sword which had been a trophy presented to Kevin Keegan. Kevin had passed it on to Bill, as a memento of their great careers together which, from Kevin's point of view, had begun so inauspiciously with him sitting on a handy dustbin while waiting to be interviewed by the great man.

The sword became a prize possession of Bill's. It is a good symbol of his attitude to the game, which had a definite 'sport is war' flavour. Some of his favourite stories bear this out, such as the one about Joe Mercer in their early football-playing days: 'There was a young man called Gordon Bremner who accidently hit Joe in the eye during a game at Hampden Park. He was disturbed about having closed Joe's eye. "Gordon," I said, "close his other bloody eye and get rid of him altogether."'

Bill also liked the ruthless nature of the story about George Hunt, who played for Bolton Wanderers before the war, and for England and Tottenham. 'He was playing at Deepdale Preston against a young goalkeeper, Jack Fairbairn, who was making his debut that day. Jack caught the ball and George was rushing in to him, so of course he stopped. George said to the young goalkeeper, "This your first game, son?" Jack thought he was going to be a little bit sympathetic, and said, "Yes," modestly. "Well, get rid of the bloody ball a bit quicker or it will be your last."'

Bill was not too proud to tell a funny story against himself, though. He liked the mental picture of himself playing one-a-side football on a hotel tennis court with Jack Dodds, another Scottish character. 'He used to come up to the hotel when my wife and I were on holiday in Blackpool every summer. And if we couldn't get a game with the waiters, we used to play one-a-side on the tennis court – fancy two grown men playing one-a-side like a couple of kids! I tell you, though, it's hard work because you have nobody to pass to. You can't get rid of the ball because if you do the opposition gets it.'

He also enjoyed telling the story of how a piece of Shankly psychological warfare went wrong. 'Cliff Basten played for Arsenal and England, and was one of the great players of all time: he scored thirty-three goals from outside left in one season. I used to play against him before the war. Every time I played against him I used to have a little bit of patter I'd go through with him. They call it motivation now, and when I hear of people talking about motivating players who are getting £600 a week, it makes my blood boil. But I had a little bit of character about me, being Scottish and brought up in the locality I was – I think your locality stamps your card for you, you know. 'Anyway, I used to be after Basten. I'd say, "Listen, if you played against *me* every week you wouldn't get many caps and you wouldn't score as many goals." I would be trying to aggravate and irritate him, and then maybe even foul him once or twice. He took no notice of me at all. In fact, he was aggravating *me*.

'During the war I met Eddie Hapgood, who used to play for Arsenal, and I said, "Listen, Eddie, remember Basten?" and he said, "Oh, yes." I said, "I used to threaten him week after week; year after year I used to threaten Basten and he took no notice of me." And Eddie said, "He wouldn't. He's stone deaf – he couldn't hear you."'

Then there is the story Joe Mercer still tells of his first meeting with the great Dixie Dean. 'When Joe Mercer went to Everton as a young boy, he was kind of skinny. The first day he stripped off in front of Dean, Dean looked at his legs and said, "Goodness gracious, Joe, if you were a postman, you wouldn't last a week!"'

Dour Hughie Gallagher's words were less picturesque, but the meaning would come over clear enough. 'Hughie played for Chelsea and Newcastle United as well as for Scotland. He was one of the most elusive men of all time. He and Alec James played together for Scotland in the great Wembley Wizards team that beat England 5–1. They did such cleverly deceptive things then, that if people saw players doing them today they would all say, "Oh, isn't it wonderful! Isn't it great!" If they *didn't* do those things before the war, we would say, "Oh, it's rubbish!"

'Anyway, Gallagher was playing at Derby one day. He had possession of the ball inside the 6-yard box and he just feinted to lean over to his left. The Derby goalkeeper went with him and dived down, and Hughie poked the ball into the opposite side of the goal, leaving him stranded on the floor. At that time there was no hugging and kissing among the players after scoring, of course. Hughie just went up to the goalkeeper and said, "Listen, son, I'll be back again." Now that's what you call character.'

Not all Bill's funny football tales were from his own playing days, naturally, though he had surprisingly few recent anecdotes to tell about the Liverpool Kop. He said he was always aware of the Kop's splendid presence behind him at any of Liverpool's home games, but concentrating too hard on what the lads were doing on the field to make mental notes of what the Kop was shouting – or singing.

He did recall some particularly delightful occasion, though, when Liverpool were playing Leeds United at Anfield. Garry Sprake was in goal. He went to throw the ball out, turned, slipped, and threw it into the back of his own goal. 'From the Kop came the instant response, right in tune, "Careless Hands". Perfect!'

Bill had another Liverpool v. Leeds story, straight from the managers' and coaches' bench. The two teams were locked in combat at Wembley for the 1965 Cup Final, which Liverpool won. 'We were sitting out in front, on a very wet day. Peter Thompson was playing for Liverpool – a very clever fellow with the ball. Leeds United are, of course, famous for their tactics, which they use to ensure that they always get a result on the day. Their outside left, the coloured player Albert Johanneson, was using all sorts of ways and means of trying to curtain Peter dribbling past Reaney, the Leeds defence player. Albert was trying to stall Peter, who had stopped in his tracks. Sid Owen said to Don Revie, "He's snookered!" Quick as a flash, Bob Paisley replied, "He's behind the black!"'

But perhaps Bill's story about the post-war Scottish international Bobbie Beattie, who also played for Preston with Bill, best sums up a good soccer player's tenacity of purpose and never-failing humour in the most adverse conditions. 'Bobbie was a really funny fellow, who happened to like a little drink . . . you know? So one day, he had drunk possibly half a flask of whisky before he went out on to the field, and when we had got as far as the passageway just on to the field, he said, "Christ, Bill, I can see two balls – I hope I kick the right one." And he did.'

And what about a soccer manager's tenacity of purpose?

Well, Bill did not entirely deny the other well-known story about how he gave his wife a real night out to celebrate their wedding anniversary by taking her to watch a Central Reserve match. 'It wasn't our wedding anniversary, it was Ness's birthday. Can you imagine me getting married in the football season?'

Jim Laker

Who will ever forget Jim Laker's wonderful feat of bowling out nineteen Aussies to win a Test series? It must have peeved him a bit that it happened at Old Trafford and not Headingley, but then Jim has always been a Yorkshireman in exile, playing for Surrey for most of his first-class cricketing days. He's one of that very rare species, the quiet Tyke – there aren't many of them about. He picks his words with the care of a compositor before he allows them to appear in public, a predilection which has made him today the perfect TV cricket commentator.

I met Jim through charity cricket. He's a big, generous man, confident in what he's achieved and expansive enough to encourage others on the way up. One of the first plays I ever wrote for TV was *Roll on 4 o'clock*. In the post the next day was a letter of congratulations from Jim Laker – and I hardly knew him then. I do now, and I value his friendship enormously.

I can't think of a better bloke in cricket to talk about the North. Jim knows all about our childhood world of 'two bat handles and a back stop with a coat', but he's also strode the hallowed halls of Lord's and Melbourne and his heavy Yorkshire tread has not always been tolerated with equanimity. Here are some of his tales.

One of Jim Laker's favourite cricket stories happened to himself in Yorkshire. A Yorkshire player was having a benefit match on a Sunday and asked Jim if he would go and play. 'Sure,' said Jim. It was a beautiful Sunday afternoon, with a crowd of about six thousand packed into the tiny ground. Laker's team went out to field first, and two local boys came out to bat. They did not do badly and made a few. Laker came on to bowl at the first change. He bowled in the friendliest manner, 'throwing them up to Jesus', to allow the lads to put on a show for the crowd. But the little fellow at the other end would have none of it. Playing in his blue cap, which everyone in Yorkshire cricket wore, he killed everything dead. After four overs, Jim was bowling slower and slower and higher and higher. Still no hits. 'At the end of four overs,' says Jim, 'I stopped the young man and said, "Come on, hit the ball and play a few shots. There's a big crowd waiting for something to happen." As an afterthought I said, "This is just like a Test match." "There's just one difference,' said the lad. "You're not getting any wickets."' Jim gave up.

Another of Jim's favourites is also about a young and inexperienced cricketer, though this time with a lot more showy confidence, who tangled with Yorkshire's great Emmott Robinson. When he was at the height of his career, Emmott was playing for Yorkshire against Cambridge at Fenners one year. Yorkshire were fielding. Emmott got someone out, and on came a nineteen-year-old playing in his first match. He was wearing a highly-coloured cap of a kind known as a 'fancy cap' in Yorkshire, where it was not liked. The lad seemed a bit full of himself, said 'Good morning' to everyone as he arrived at the wicket and said something to Emmott which upset him a little. Emmott's first ball was magnificent and knocked the off stump out of the ground. 'My word, Emmott,' said the lad, 'that was a good ball!' 'Aye, lad, it was, and it were wasted on thee.'

There is another Emmott Robinson story in Jim's repertoire, this one involving Neville Cardus, who first told it. Emmott was run out when about to save the match, playing in mid-July. He never spoke again for months. In the following February, Cardus encountered him in the street. There was snow on the ground, and there was this little figure, in a cloth cap, hands in pockets, looking down at the ground as he walked along. Cardus came up alongside: 'How are you? Wintering well?' Emmott looked up: 'Aye, Mr Cardus. I never should have done it, I never should have done it.' Perhaps Emmott was thinking of how censorious the Yorkshire crowd could have been about his mistake, for in those days the crowd was considerably less mellow than it is today. Even in the late sixties, they could give a tough time to a player of whom they disapproved, as in Jim's story about Keith Fletcher and Fred Trueman.

When Keith Fletcher played in his first Test match in Yorkshire in 1968, he had been picked in preference to the Yorkshire player Phil Sharpe. He got the bird all day and missed three catches – probably difficult ones, but the Yorkshire supporters were convinced Sharpe would have got them. Several years later, on the infamous occasion in 1975 when the Headingley pitch was desecrated before the start of the last day of an Australian Test match, Jim Laker was called to Headingley. He walked out to the middle where Fred Trueman was there with several others looking in horror at the pitch. One man looked at Fred and said, 'What would you do with this guy?' 'Send him to prison for twenty years for desecrating the pitch.' 'That's a bit harsh. How about a re-think?' 'All right. I'd take him up to the top of that Rugby League stand there, and I'd drop him, and I'd have Fletcher underneath to catch him.'

Fred also figures in another story Jim tells, this time about the Third Test against the West Indies at Trent Bridge in 1957. Peter May was the England captain who, with the scent of victory up his nose, had enforced the follow-on. With West Indies at 89 for 5 and players of the calibre of Worrell, Sobers, Walcott, Kanhai and Weekes all back in the pavilion, things looked good for England. Then Collie Smith began putting together a remarkable innings. He even played Statham, the Lancashire fast bowler, off the back foot into the pavilion. He was safely into three figures when the second new ball was due. Fred was going to take it, even though his strength had begun to wane in the battle against Collie Smith. The crowd had noticed this and someone shouted, 'Fred, you're no quicker than bloody Laker,' which brought and angry glare and a curse from Fred. He bowled three perfect outswingers, and Collie played and missed all three. Fred stood in the middle of the pitch, arms akimbo, took a few seconds to get his breath back, then said, 'Smith, going to Bloody Ireland tomorrow are you? Tha's no need for thee to fly – tha can bloody walk there.'

Fred Trueman, breathing fire and smoke, was straight out of the 'sport as war' branch of the game. Not so George Hirst, whom Jim likes to quote: 'There's nowt like a game of cricket, lad. I said "a game". Cricket was never made for any championship . . . cricket's a game, not a competition.'

Nor is Fred much like that quiet, modest Yorkshireman, Wilfred Rhodes who, aged ninety, was dubbed 'Lord's Taverners Cricketer of the Century'. Responding, Rhodes said, 'I allus enjoyed the game of cricket. It were a bit of a hobby of mine.' (He had scored 40,000 runs and taken 4,000 wickets in pursuit of his 'hobby'.)

Hirst and Rhodes were from an age when cricket was quieter, and the rewards were in personal satisfaction, not money. Even when Jim Laker began playing in the Yorkshire League, there still existed the custom of taking round the hat for a player who reached the age of fifty. The old players, of forty-five or so, could look round the ground and tell to a shilling what they would get – usually about £4 or £5.

But let's end on a Laker favourite about the top end of cricket in Yorkshire. This one is about Brian Sellers, Yorkshire's finest captain in the 1930s. In his first match as captain, Yorkshire were playing MCC at Lord's. He arrived early with his father (who was on the Yorkshire committee). It had rained quite heavily in the night and Sellers and his father went out at about 9.30 to look at the wicket. Later, when he went out to toss, he won and put MCC in to bat. At lunch, they were 130 for 0. As the team went back up the pavilion steps, one of them said to Sellers, 'What made thee put 'em in, then?' Sellers said, 'I looked at the wicket with my father and he said it was the best thing to do.' 'Well, you'd better go and get your bloody father to come on and bowl them out!'

Arthur Clues

In the early fifties I used to watch Warrington Rugby League Club avidly. We had a forward, an Australian rhinocerous, called Harry Bath. He was the best, most agile, powerful second-row in the world save one: Arthur Clues. Arthur played for Leeds but *with* Bath for Australia. As a duo they were invincible. They were the forerunners of today's speedy, neat-handling, creative forwards, but giants of men to boot. And Arthur, happy, jovial and outspoken, knew his worth.

After a year at Leeds, having lifted them to the top of their division, broken the club's try-scoring record, and opened up hitherto uncharted territories in forward play, he went to see the chairman – a hard, no-nonsense Northern industrialist of the old school. Arthur, forthright as ever, laid before the boss his achievements for the club, spelt them out in detail and demanded more money. The chairman nodded and leaned back in his chair. 'You're right, Arthur,' he said, 'you been worth your weight in gold to this club. You're the best signing we've ever made and there's no doubt in my mind that anything we've achieved this season is entirely due to your example, influence and efforts.' 'Right,' said Arthur pleased, 'how much rise do I get?' 'Nowt!' said the chairman – and he *didn't*.

Arthur married a Yorkshire girl and settled in Leeds where he's become an influential character in all the city's sporting circles. There's no big occasion at Headingley without 'Big A' – like Bill Shankly he's an alien who fell in love with the North and he's only too willing to talk about his long-lasting affair.

Arthur Clues, huge, young, innocent and a very promising Rugby League player, arrived in England from sunny Australia in the middle of winter, 1947, the worst in living memory. It was something of a shock, but he settled in well at Leeds, where the Rugby League Club had invited him over from his home country, and where he still lives. He even got himself photographed for the local newspapers eating snow with obvious enjoyment. Newspapers were soon noticing him for other reasons.

'The first time I played against Wigan at Wigan, Ken Gee, who was a great player, was in their team. I was always having a tussle on the field with Gee or Joe Egan. Gee was playing, we were leading, and I was having a pretty good game, when he came and hit me with one of these stiff-arm tackles. He was more or less strangling me, and so I bit him to make him release his hold on me. There was only about five minutes left at Central Park, and as he was walking off the field he turned back and shouted, "Look, look at what the big bugger did, the big Australian bugger," and he showed all the teeth marks to the referee, who sent me off as well for biting. When we were walking back through the little tunnel to the dressing room I said, "Why did you do that, you big soft Pommie so-and-so?" He said, "Well, I'd been sent off so I thought I'd better get thee sent off, lad, as well." Anyway, he got a four-match suspension, and I got two for biting. Eddie Waring wrote an article in the *Sunday Mirror*: "Australian international now playing for Leeds sent off for biting . . ." There it was on the front page of a national paper, written by Eddie Waring, and saying, "When man bites dog, that's not news; when dog bites man, that's not news; but when man bites man, that's Clues." I got a lot of stick around Leeds for that.'

It is said with a roar of laughter. Despite the still-noticeable Australian accent, Arthur is now very definitely a Northerner, and tells his stories of life in Yorkshire with great relish.

'There was another game against Wigan, when the scrum collapsed. Egan kicked me straight in the eye, and I had to have about nine stitches in it. I heard a voice saying, "Look, you big Australian so-an-so, don't go down in the scrum in England," in a Lancastrian accent. I never said a word, just went straight off and got my eye stitched up, and when I came back on the field, I never had a go at him. But about two years later we were playing again at Headingley and the scrum collapsed, and there was Joe Egan's head, so I kicked him straight in the mush and broke his nose in about four places. At the same time, I said, "Look, you Pommie bastard, never go down in a scrum in England." Every time I see Joe we often talk about that incident and laugh.'

Arthur looks on those days of Northern rugby league in the late forties and fifties as good days. There were a lot of personalities in the game then. 'Brian Bevans, for instance, was magic, the greatest winger I've ever seen in my life. He had no teeth, he was bald, he had sticking plaster round his knees. I used to call him the skeleton in braces, but he scored tries out of this world – tries that you wouldn't dream about. He scored seventy-odd tries in one season, about nine or ten of them in one match, but he never looked as if he could. He used to chain smoke, was always spitting and snorting. Every time we went to France with Other Nationalities [a team of Irish, Australian and Scots players] Bev used always to room with me. I used to take a little alarm clock with me, and Bev would take his teeth out and put them in a glass, and I'd be reaching out, half-asleep in the morning, to the alarm, and pulling these teeth out, and he'd be sitting there, smoking and spitting at five o'clock in the morning . . . an absolute freak as a footballer.

'There was a little hunchback referee, called Laurie Thorpe, from Leeds. He was a very fair fellow. I got a thump one day playing at Headingley. He saw the bloke do it, and he didn't caution him, but he knew I would give the bloke one back later on. When I did, he pulled me over in front of all the stands – and we used to average about 30,000 people in those days – and started digging me in the chest. He wasn't that big, Laurie, but he used to pick on big fellows, and dig you in the chest, to make sure that he was superior. He said, "Big A, they think I am giving you a bollocking, but you did right in hitting that bastard – he hit you first." The crowd was screaming, thinking he was going to send me off.

'I played cricket for Leeds for about ten years, and had two seasons with Freddie Trueman. He was in the Air Force then, and I used to field at short leg with him. One day, there was a bit of a soft wicket at Halifax; Geoff Carr was one of the bowlers, with Freddie opening second at the other end. Our Captain, Michael Crawford, was the captain of Yorkshire's Second, went to Oxford, and spoke with a rather pukka accent. Freddie was in the leg slip and I was second leg slip to this Geoff Carr. The batsman hit Geoff for a couple of fours, and Freddie said, "When I get you up t'other end, I'll pin you against bluddy sight screen!" He was cursing and swearing at this fellow, who reported him to the umpire. Michael Crawford said (posh accent), "Ah, Freddie, we've had enough of this swearing. You know you are not allowed to talk to people when the bowler is coming up to bowl to them." Freddie replied, "I can always go back to t'bluddy pit, tha knows . . ." Then he turned to me and said, "We'll take the lot on after the game." He wanted to fight the whole team, did Trueman. "Look Freddie," I said, "I've got a reputation as a nice fella, you know. I don't want to get taken up with eleven other blokes." "We'll do the bluddy lot, thee and me," was the reply. A great player, Freddie.'

Once his playing days were over, Arthur opened a sports goods shop in Leeds. He was now a prominent citizen of the city, and his shop became a landmark. People from all over the place, from as far away as Australia, would drop in to look him up. Sometimes total strangers would find their way to his house, perhaps because they had been given directions by cricketing rugby-playing Australians to whom the Clues family had given hospitality. Arthur used always to put on a party for the Australian cricket team when they were in Leeds.

Once Arthur and his wife were sitting in the back garden on a Sunday morning, doing a bit of sun-bathing, when forty Australians turned up in six London taxis. 'There must have been eight of them in each taxi. Anyway, there they were at the front door. "Good day, Cluesie, you are the only one around here we know with a shower. Can we have a bloody shower, mate? We've got letters of introduction from so-an-so." They had been sleeping in the hedge bottoms, and they all stank to high heaven. Where they came from, I don't know. I did not know any of them. There was a surge of bodies and packs all over the house. My wife got a bit fed up – she had to make them all coffee and feed them. But they all got showers.'

Ernie Clay

Ernie Clay is living out of his time. He's Dickensian – a larger-than-life, big-voiced, self-made man from working-class Leeds, who now lives in Southern luxury in a big house and has champagne for tea. When I asked him what it meant to be that rich he said, 'We can have grapes in the house when nobody's ill.' But by God he enjoys life, enjoys doing outrageous things, like dumping a hairy-arsed Rugby League team in the quiet streets of football-loving Fulham. He's like a breath of fresh air wherever he goes – people automatically fall in behind him, sucked in by the vacuum his presence leaves in its wake. He's a big Northern character with a big laugh. He's ruthless, demands value for his money both in time and effort – but he loves people, can be tight one minute and supremely generous the next.

Ernie always has a lot to say. What has he to say about Northern humour?

Ernie Clay thinks that to get the best out of the type of humour characteristic of Northerners, you have to have someone you can bounce your jokes and cracks off, someone who will respond in kind. When he first moved South more than twenty-five years ago, he found that people thought him cheeky and saucy; the great Northern insult did not go down too well with people who did not know that they were expected to come back with a crack of their own. These days, however, people will reply in kind when he walks down the street in Fulham, calling a cheery good morning to everyone, where once they would have thought him very odd, but he still finds that he does not go into his neighbours' houses unless there has been a tragedy.

It's all so different up North. 'People think we are inquisitive up there. But we're not. We are really ensuring that we know how everyone around is getting on. If anyone's ill we'll all know and be able to help. Really and truly, you live in a community up there.

'The Northern joke? Well, that's a way of breaking down the barrier between strangers, isn't it? Like when I go into the Inland Revenue office and say to the girl, "Now, I don't want any shooting match this week!"

'Mind you, you mustn't forget the wind up North! When I was a lad, and we were having it so hard in the industrial North, the London Cockneys may have been having it hard too, but what they didn't have was the bloody wind blowing up from Derbyshire through South Yorkshire and freezing you to death! You have to talk, to joke, to keep going.'

Wind or no wind, it is still the community thing – everyone being equal – that Ernie thinks is paramount in making North-Country people the way they are. 'When I go up North these days, I go home in my Rolls-Royce – bought from the same yard where I used to wash cars for 6d a time back in the late twenties. Being a fat fellow, I can eat fish and chips and mushy peas and all that. Up there, I always go to all the fish restaurants there are. Everyone will tell you, "There's a new one open – you must try that." Come the end of the day, you go to Harry Ramsden's and all those places; outside, as well as your own car, there will be ruddy donkeys and carts, lorries, gypsies and rich supermarket owners, and you all sit down to eat your fish and chips and mushy peas together. You are queuing up for them like everybody else, and it doesn't matter a blooming thing who you are. You are there by your own rights.'

Ernie tells many stories of the generosity of Northerners and the welcome they'll give to strangers. Like the time he was taking some of the Fulham people up to Wigan for a match, and the car broke down. Someone came from a nearby garage and helped them, and wouldn't take anything for his services. 'The fellow just said, "That'll be all right. Come on, we'll go to t'pub." And the landlord there said to us, "Next time you cum oop here, if you're in t'second division still, let us know, and we'll cut you some sandwiches."'

In splendid contrast is Ernie's story of the time the joke was definitely on him. 'We were having a meeting of Fulham's directors. Len Shackleton, Bertie Mee, Alec Stock, and Ted Drake from Southampton were all there. Shack had come from up North and had to go back that day. We decided we needed a couple of centre forwards. As we were coming out of the meeting Len Shackleton said he could probably help with the forwards. "I can give you a couple of numbers; ring them and they'll help." Anyway, I drove him back to Gatwick for his flight, and as he was going through he said again, "Don't forget those numbers." "Shall I mention your name?" I asked. "Mention my name if you like, though when you ring you will have no need to." "Leave it to me," I shouted as he disappeared through the door.

'I went back to my secretary and told her to ring these two numbers and say we want two strikers. I went back to her later and asked if she had rung them. "Well, I did and I didn't," she said. "What do you mean? You've either done it or you haven't?" I said. "Give me the bloody phone and I'll do it." So I rang the first of the numbers, and I suddenly realized that I knew them. I was ringing Arthur Scargill and the National bloody Coal Board in Barnsley! Now that's the sort of humour I like. I could have killed Shack, mind you, but I liked it.'

Sports Shorts

We can't leave Northern sport without digging into the veritable mine of anecdotes and comments that have found their way into print over the years. How many of them are fact or mere legend is neither here nor there: they help us to complete our picture of that unique, highly competitive, dry-witted animal, the Great Northern Athlete.

Who better to start with than the late, great Neville Cardus, born and brought up in Manchester and one of the finest and most elegant of cricket writers? The first three pieces I have chosen here, from three different books, were all collected into an anthology, *Cardus in the Covers*, published a few years ago.

To set the scene, here is a picture of Whitsuntide at Old Trafford, which first apeared in *Days in the Sun*:

. . . This crowd, indeed, is something more than the sum total of the individuals in it; it has a being of its own; it was born in the dim past and will outlive us all. Man and boy, this crowd has been going to Old Trafford in Whit Week these fifty years; man and boy, it will be going there in thrice fifty years to come. A crowd is of immense humanity, and on a warm day the mellowness of sunshine enters into the ranks. Talk of the hard, grinding North, ignorant Southerner – poor man, have you never seen Old Trafford settling down after lunch, all of us huddled intimately, basking in the afternoon's light, the old pavilion seeming to drowse? The rigour of the game is appreciated keenly enough by Old Trafford's crowd, but it is in its most lovable moment towards a golden day's fall, just as the play gets a little stale and attention on the cricketers begins to dwindle. Then the multitude seeks for amusement of its own making, and now's the time for men of humour. A policeman is walking in dignity along the boundary's edge. The crowd suddenly sees him with one eye. And with a single voice chant the packed thousands: 'Left, right! Left, right!' keeping time to the solemn movements of the policeman, who endeavours hard to seem utterly oblivious that a cynosure is being made of him. In this hour of Old Trafford's 'sweet doing nothing' have you ever heard the crowd entertain itself by singing to two-part harmony a ditty about 'Down by the Ohio'? A good time to have the ears ravished by this musical performance is in the middle of an interminable partnership against Lancashire's bowling, when some impregnable bats have seemingly put the game to a standstill. Then is it that music is made to soothe Old Trafford's breast: 'Down by the Ohio', with a cadence of linked sweetness long drawn out, goes into the mild air. And after the protracted dying away of that cadence the crowd, as a man, applauds its own waggish self. 'Hooray!' it says, laughing the broadest laugh that ever was. Does a wicket fall at last? Very well, Old Trafford now loosens it legs. 'Up! Up! Up!' the multitude chants, and every man jack of them stands up. Does a new batsman come in? Very well, again; the multitude chants, 'Down! Down! Down!' and down once more it sits. Behold Old Trafford's crowd in this hour of its content and call the critic a fool who talks of the unbending North and its economic man.

From *Second Innings* comes this story of disaster in Leeds one August Bank Holiday. Yorkshire, apparently all set for a comfortable win, needed only 50 after Lancashire's second innings had collapsed so that they were all out just before close of play. Next day, the ground had few visitors, 'except those necessary to go through the formalities attendant upon obtaining the correct statistics of a ten-wicket victory for Yorkshire'. Here's what actually happened.

Gentle rain in the night had made the turf capricious, and before we knew what was happening the Yorkshire innings fell into rack and ruin. When the last batsman was overwhelmed and Lancashire had really and truly won the match, I rushed from the ground, eager to carry the good news back to Manchester. I leapt on a tram, sat down inside, and the guard came with his tickets. 'What's they won by – lost any wickets gettin' them?' I told him that Lancashire, not Yorkshire, were the victors. He expressed some impatience. 'Ah'm talking about t'cricket,' he said, presumably under the impression I had come straight from a polo match or archery tournament. I repeated to him the dreadful truth, and he suspended business at once. He didn't give me a ticket but turned his back on me and walked from the almost empty tram, conveyed the news to a trolleyboy, who relayed it to the driver. The tram proceeded to travel some three miles into Leeds by its own volition.

When I reached the railway station, I was a little in advance of the departure of the train to Manchester, so I entered a refreshment-room and sat down at a little table. Shortly afterwards, a man sat down next to me, in cap and muffler, and spoke in the speech of Laisterdyke. 'Eh, dear,' he said, 'who'd 'a' thowt it? Faa-ncy Yorkshire crackin' oop like that. Ah'd never 'a' thowt it.' There was no anger in his voice, no tone of abuse directed at the faltering Yorkshire eleven. There was only the accent of sorrow. 'Eh, dear,' he repeated, 'it's a rum 'un.' He eyed me carefully, then said, 'Tha doesn't seem to be takin' this very much to 'eart,' and I was obliged to explain to him that, as I came from Lancashire and Manchester, born and bred there, I couldn't be expected to 'take it to heart' exactly. He looked at me from a different angle.

'So tha'rt from Lankysheer art tha, eh, dear; and tha's from Lankysheer?'

'Yes, from Lancashire.'

A slight pause.

'And tha's coom all way from Manchester to watch match, ast tha?'

'Yes, that's it,' I answered.

'And tha's goin' back to Manchester by two-twenty train, eh?'

Yes, I told him, I was indeed returning to my native city by the two-twenty train. After another short spell of meditation, he said:

'Tha'll be feelin' very pleased with thisell, won't thi'?'

'Naturally,' I replied, taking care not to look too triumphant.

'Eh, by gum. Faa-ncy Yorksheer crackin' like that. Aye. Tha'll be feelin' very pleased with thisell. Ah shouldn't wonder.'

And he repeated the question:

'And tha's goin' back to Manchester by two-twenty train, art tha'?'

Feeling now a little access of irritation, I answered:

'Yes, straight back.'

'Well,' he said, without the slightest heat, 'Ah 'opes tha drops down dead before tha gets there.'

Cardus could write as well – and as lovingly – about village cricket as he could about the great set pieces of county cricket or test matches. The following story comes from *The Summer Game:*

. . . The captain of the village team is the village parson; every week he opens the innings with Simpson, his gardener. And every week, without exception, the Rev. P. P. Jenkins goes to the wicket believing that somehow he is about to play, at last, the innings of his life. He hits his first ball for four, a stroke which is impressive because of its great power and rashness. He attempts a like stroke from the second ball and he is comprehensively bowled. As he departs from the wicket Simpson, his gardener, says, 'Aye, but Maister Jenkins 'e does have a terrible shortness of patience for a minister of the Church.' And laughter that makes for fellow-feeling is born forthwith.

Hobbs and Sutcliffe stealing runs against a swift field – an admirable sight this, but where's the humour of it? as Corporal Nye would ask. We do not laugh at the thing that is well done. Watch the Rev. P. P. Jenkins and his curate as they steal *their* runs. The curate plays a ball nervously towards cover and cried out 'Yes – No?', an ambiguous remark which leaves the Rev. P. P. Jenkins suspended, so to speak, in thin air, mid-wicket. Frantically he doubles on his tracks, flings himself along the earth and gets home by the skin of his teeth. He picks himself up; his heart returns from his mouth to its proper place. He looks down the pitch at his apologetic curate and says, choosing words with much self-control. 'My dear Tompkinson, do try to be definite. I hate a "Yes – No"; it is very confusing.'

The Rev. P. P. Jenkins could have benefited from another Cardus anecdote, reprinted in the *Guardian* just after Herbert Sutcliffe died in January 1978:

> Well did he [Sutcliffe] know, better than most batsmen, that there is a time to make strokes and a time to abstain from making them. At Sheffield, one sun-burnt afternoon, just after the 1914–18 War, he was handsomely immobile through a succession of maiden overs. A friendly voice from the crowd asked him, 'What dost think tha art, Herbert? A ruddy war memorial?'

There is another Cardus anecdote about the deadly seriousness of cricket when played between Yorkshire and Lancashire which has been repeated in various forms by various people. Here it is, as Cardus wrote it in his *Autobiography*: 'Roy Kilner, Yorkshire to the end of his days and for ever after, once said that umpires were only "luxurious superfluities" in a Lancashire and Yorkshire match. "They gets in t'way. What we want in Yarksheer and Lankysheer matches is 'fair dos' – no umpires, and honest cheatin' all round, in conformity with the law."'

That's the sort of open, honest attitude which gave rise to the legend, still current, that if a Roses match were played at Bramall Lane, the word could soon go round Sheffield's factories: 'Stoke up chimneys: Lancashire's batting.'

Northern sporting legend is full of stories of the great names of cricket, but probably few players have had as many stories told about them as Fred Trueman. Fred himself says that most of them are aprocryphal, but there is no denying that his own ready wit and his activities on and off the field have had a lot to do with the creation of the legend. One such story is the one recounted by Fred Rumsey in *The Thoughts of Trueman Now*, a book in which Fred was heavily involved himself, and he doesn't deny it.

The MCC were touring Australia. Fred and the Reverend David Sheppard were both in the team, and the latter was generally met at airports by others of his calling. On one occasion at Sydney, the plane was met by a bishop and a nun. Fred, from the rear of the aircraft was heard to call to the Reverend David at the front, 'Eh-up, Rev, not only has the senior pro. come to meet you, but he's fixed you up as well.'

Here's another tale which bears witness to Trueman's humour, its authenticity vouched for by the writer A. A. Thomson, who was told it by a captain of Hampshire. Thomson repeated it in his book *Anatomy of Laughter*:

> It was in a game of briskly competitive declarations and Yorkshire were finally set a formidable task for victory. This they proceeded to attack with vigour. Freddie was doing his utmost to score quickly and in order to keep him quiet the Hampshire captain brought into action a slow bowler who favoured a high trajectory. He, in fact, pitched the ball so well up that Freddie, eager to hit it out of sight, kept on missing it altogether.
>
> After two overs of these ferocious near-misses, the fielding captain strolled across with a word of sympathy.
>
> 'What's the matter, Freddie? Why don't you hit him?'
>
> 'He chucks 'em up so far in the air,' retorted Freddie, 'that, by the time they come down, I'm bang out of form!'

Fred Trueman himself told this story in *The Thoughts of Trueman Now*:

> When I was in the RAF I played with that wonderful man, Alan Shirreff. He was our captain. He always had a little something against Yorkshiremen but I could never

find out what it was till one night after a few drinks he told me. When he was a young man at Cambridge University before the war he was in the Cambridge side; they were playing against Yorkshire and Shirreff was batting. Behind the wickets was a character by the name of Arthur Wood, who was a wonderful joker. At first slip was one of the best slip fielders I have ever seen, Arthur Mitchell. As Alan Shirreff took his guard, he said, 'Good morning.' They said, 'Good morning.' The first ball he received was from the great left-arm slow bowler Hedley Verity. He pushed the ball back with a straight defensive bat and Arthur Wood was heard to say: 'Very good shot, young man, that looked very good indeed, what a lovely defensive shot.' The next ball he did the same and again, 'That was a very good shot indeed, young man.' Now that one was with an even straighter bat and he turned to Arthur Mitchell, and said, 'Ticker [which was his nickname], what did you think of that?' 'Yes,' said Arthur, 'yes, it looked very good indeed, nice straight bat, the hand not too far round the top, very nice indeed.' So Alan Shirreff thought, 'These Yorkshiremen aren't so bad.' A couple of balls later, a little bolder, Alan went down the track to play a ball pitched a little wider. Of course, Hedley Verity had seen him coming, turned it a little more, he missed it and Arthur Wood had the bails off in a flash and said, 'Now bugger off back there where you belong and tell your mates to get in here quick, we've got a train to catch.' So Alan's attitude to Yorkshire is now understandable.

Football also provides many a laugh up North, though some of the best come not from players, but from the spectators. There are many stories told about the wondrous wit of the Liverpool Kop, for instance. You will have found a few scattered about in this book already, amongst the recollections of men like Lawrie McMenemy and Bill Shankly. Here is another well-known one, which was also a favourite of Bill's. It takes place on a foggy day at Anfield when Liverpool were playing a Cup tie against Walsall. Eventually, the ground became so enveloped in fog that spectators at one end of the ground could not see the other. Then, away in the murk, someone scored a goal at the Anfield Road end. Instantly, the Kop began to chant: 'Who scored the goal? Who scored the goal?' Back came the reply: 'Tony Hateley scored, Tony Hateley scored.' Then from the Kop, to the tune of the current hit 'Aintree Iron', came: 'Thank you very much for the information.'

Then there was another cup game, Liverpool versus Bury, when Liverpool were not doing too well, and decided on a substitution. Fairclough was substituted for Johnson, a move which the Kop clearly thought poorly of, for their reaction was a resounding chant of: 'We all agree, Tiswas is better than Swap Shop.'

The police usually find themselves targets for the Kop wit during Liverpool matches. I remember a time when a mounted policeman fell off his horse, and the Kop began singing: 'Do You Think We Would Leave You Lying There . . .?' And I once watched two policemen, walking side by side in step past the Kop, trying to remain apparently unconscious of the Kop's derisive whistling of the famous Laurel and Hardy signature tune.

Even away from home, the Liverpool wit remains undimmed. A contribution by Ken Dodd to *A Legend in His Own Time*, a tribute to Bill Shankly when he retired in 1974, was this story of Liverpudlians at Wembley:

> One Cup Final thousands surged around the ground and Wembley Way. In full control of the situation was a mounted policeman, a magnificent sight . . . click, click, click went his tongue as he contemptuously moved along the thousands of Liverpudlians . . . his scorn for these Northern fans plain for all to see.
>
> But he was destroyed in a second. Clap, clap, clap went the fans, 'Lester Piggott' they chanted. His face went the colour of a Liverpool shirt as he rode away muttering some very choice Metropolitan obscenities.

Tommy Docherty tells another Cup Final story. The day his club, Manchester United, played Southampton in the 1976 Final, he went down to the hotel barber's shop for a shave. This cost only 50p. United lost, and on the Monday after the Final, Docherty went into a local shop near Old Trafford to be tidied up again. This time the barber asked for £3. Docherty couldn't believe it and told him a shave had cost him only 50p in London. 'Ah,' said the barber, quick as a flash, 'but your face is longer today!'

And it was witty Docherty who once said to centre forward Stuart Pearson, complaining of a bad back after a hard training session: 'Don't worry, son. Manchester City have got two!'

Talking of Manchester City, several comedians have told versions of the following story. Malcolm Allison came out of Main Road, big cigar in mouth, and saw a little coloured lad kicking the ball on his toe, on his knee, on his shoulder, and back down, flicking it back. He was really good and only nine years

121

old. Malcolm said, 'Tell you what I'll do with you, you're a very clever little fellow, I'll sign you for Manchester City.' And the little lad said, 'Get knotted – it's bad enough being black!'

To end on a golfing note, here's a story from Jimmy Tarbuck about the golfer who was always accompanied by his dog when playing a round. Every time the golfer made a good shot or sank a long putt, the dog would stand up on his hind legs and applaud his master with his front paws. A friend asked him what the dog did when the golfer landed in a bunker or missed an easy putt. 'Oh,' said the golfer, 'he turns somersaults.' 'How many?' asked the friend. 'It depends on how hard I kick him up the arse,' came the reply.

Postscript: A throwaway line from Eric Morecambe I'd be sorry for you to go through life without knowing – 'The greatest fielder I ever knew caught everything and had to be sent home half-way through the series.'

Nicknames

We all love nicknames. It's not particularly Northern – the Cockneys are brilliant at it – but from what I remember of the names we used to nick, there was an element of ironic humour about them which was endemic to the playgrounds of southwest Lancashire.

Potters were always 'Pansies', of course, Tates invariably 'Spuds', and all Gordons 'Flash'. But there were others who'll carry their nicknames to their graves with, I suspect, pride, as a testament to their unique juvenile popularity.

'Nigs' Blake was so called because of an ever so slight sallowness of skin – who'd heard of racial sensitivity? 'Smokey' Jackson could always be found in the lavs pulling on a fag. 'Cus' Jackson's name was Eric – we studied Latin – hence Ericus. An academic 'education' wasn't wasted. 'Rouggie' was a redhead, *après rouge* – and a lad who always seemed up on all the scandal was dubbed 'Reuter' – or 'Rewter' as our untrained tongues used to shape it.

Girls were fair game, too; we were co-ed. All lasses called Ball were christened 'Eva' – to heave meant to throw. No need to enlarge on 'Bum Bum' Lloyd . . . and 'Titty' Simpson remains affectionately warm and indelible in my memory.

Our nickname policy was usually compassionate. Very rarely were squints or other physical disabilities ever dwelt upon . . . 'Boat' Harris had enormous feet and 'Congo' Cripps was a pretty hulking brute, but neither minded. Fran Cotton, later to become the great British Lions and England Rugby Union prop, was always 'Dan' after 'Desperate' and it stuck with him into the Halls of Fame.

But we were civilized and never more than to a lad who must have been saddled with the most unfortunate initials ever. His name was Bason, and his initials: W.C.! Really! Honest! . . . and we called him 'Bill'!

Most other Northern nicknames fall into four categories, depending on their association with work, food, sport, or the

Northerner's sense of humour, which may be gentle, but is more likely to be ironic, sarcastic or withering.

In the 'work' category, you are likely to encounter the following nicknames for towns and their inhabitants:

Birmingham: 'Bangalore', because of the many Asians who arrived in the 1960s to work in the textile industry.

Bradford: 'Gateway to the East', for the same reason as above.

Darwen: 'Darren Artillery' ('Darren' being the dialect pronunciation of Darwen). According to Bob Dobson, author of a splendid book on Lancashire nicknames, this refers to the sound of the weavers' clog irons and soles as they hurried to the mills over the flagstones. The clogs themselves were called artillery because the men used them as weapons in fights.

Denton: 'Hatters'. They made hats there.

Haslingdon: 'T'capital of Asia Minor'. Another reference to the Asian workers in the cotton mills.

Horwich: 'Horwich Locos', referring not to madness, but to the trains and railway industry.

Warrington: 'Wires', because of the wire manufactured in the town.

Nicknames arising from food cover all sorts of situations. In Manchester, for instance, where they call greengrocers and grocers 'moonrakers', they also call them 'split currants' because they are supposed to be so mean that they will split a currant to get the weight exactly right. A few others are:

Accrington: 'Accrington Shotheads'. The shothead (or Billhead, or Miller's Thumb) is a small fish with a big head, and the reference is to the Accringtonians' supposed big-headedness.

Bury: 'Black Puddings'.

Darwen: 'Darren selmon', a sarcastic reference to the extreme pollution of the River Darwen, which has ensured that there have been no salmon found in it since the Industrial Revolution.

Eccles: 'Cakes', an obvious one.

Everton: 'Toffeemen'. Even the national newspapers have referred to the players of Everton FC as 'toffeemen'. The nickname arises from the fame achieved by the toffee made by an

Everton woman, Milly Bushnell, way back in the eighteenth century. It was once the nickname of Everton natives and is now that of the football club, whose mascot is Milly Bushnell.

Liverpool: 'Scouse' and 'scousers'. A favourite dish among Liverpudlians has long been a type of potato hash called 'lobscouse'. Shortened to 'scouse', it is now a familiar nickname for Liverpudlians and their dialect.

Incidentally, 'Bolton Trotters', the nickname of Bolton Wanderers FC, does *not* refer to pigs' trotters. Bob Dobson says it grew out of the dialect verb 'to trot', meaning to hoax, tease, make fun of people, or pull their legs.

Most Northern football and Rugby League clubs have a nickname, usually referring to the colour of their strip, to a local industry or product, or to a team's past exploits. Here is the Rugby Football League's official list of club nicknames:

Barrow: Shipbuilders
Batley: Gallant Youths (they won four cups, *c.* 1897)
Blackpool Boroughs: Seasiders
Bradford Northern: Northern
Bramley: Villagers
Cardiff: Blue Dragons
Castleford: Glassblowers
Doncaster: Dons
Featherstone Rovers: Colliers
Halifax: Thrum Hallers
Huddersfield: Fartowners
Hull: Airlie Birds (sometimes Early Birds)
Hull Kingston Rovers: The Robins
Huyton: Ton
Keighley: Lawkholmers
Leeds: Loiners
Oldham: Roughyeds
Rochdale Hornets: Nets
St Helens: Saints
Salford: Red Devils
Swinton: Lions
Wakefield Trinity: Dreadnoughts
Warrington: Wires

Whitehaven: Haven
Widnes: Chemics
Wigan: Riversiders
Workington Town: Town
York: Wasps

I always wondered why they called them the Grigthorpe tiddlers.

Fulham, one of the newest clubs in the League, whose home is on the Thames in South-West London, would also like to be called the Riversiders but, inevitably, they are getting called Cockneys up North.

Among the many nicknames which have grown out of the Northerner's sense of humour are:

Batley: 'T'suntrap of the North'. Heavy irony, this, on a par with the old joke about how the birds have to fly backwards in Batley to keep the soot out of their eyes.

Blackpool: 'Sand-grown 'uns'. There's a nice seaside air about this one. It used to refer just to people born in Blackpool, but has been taken up by people from all along the Lancashire coast, from Liverpool to Morecambe.

Bury: 'Bury Muffs'. Bob Dobson thinks this probably originated from cock-fighting, as a hen's crest is called a muff. In dialect, to 'marry muff' means 'talk nonsense'.

Chorley: 'Petty-door bangers'. Bob Dobson has traced this derisive term back to the 1930s, and it may be older. It seems to have some lewd connection with the lavatory. Another nickname for Chorley natives is 'mallet-heads'. According to tradition, Chorley people are a bit thick because all Chorley children receive a bang on the head with a mallet at birth.

Clifton: 'Gawpers'. Bob Dobson has dug up an alleged peculiarity of the people of Clifton to account for this one. It seems that when a Clifton villager saw a stranger in the street outside, he would bang his cupboard door as a signal to the neighbour to go and have a look or 'gawp' at him.

Lancashire: 'Sprawngers'. A sprawnger was a village storyteller, most of his stories being humorous.

Oswaldtwistle: 'Gobbinland', from the dialect term 'gobbin', meaning a slow-witted person.

The Rustic North

If you were to ask me for the main difference between the average Lancashireman and his Yorkshire counterpart, I would say immediately (if there is such a word): rusticity. Every Yorkshireman, even if born and bred in the heart of Leeds or Bradford, has one foot in a field. Nowhere in Yorkshire are you more than a hop, skip and a jump from open country, most of it beautiful, and most of its inhabitants rural in the extreme. They're often dour, self-interested and paranoically conscious of their parochial identity.

The Lancashireman, on the other hand, is an urban animal. Most of the population of Lancashire are either big-city dwellers or lost in the massive urban sprawl of the south-west of the county. This breeds a different character altogether – slick, quick-witted, self-depreciating. Liverpudlians, for instance, would hardly admit to being Lancastrians at all – while Manchester men have deserted their county cricket pride to howl the praise of their *city* at the Stretford end of Maine Road.

And so it's mainly from Yorkshire – at least from its rural majority – that a special brand of Northern humour has risen and is still expounded. It paints the picture of the Northerner as cynical ancient, his words, in rich dialect, falling out of his mouth, dealing contemptuously with the idiot Southerner who happens to pass his way. He is wise, down-to-earth, always comes out on top. He populates a world that existed only in the minds of the Yorkshire myth-makers like the writers of Emmerdale Farm. I deplore him, his type of humour and comedians who perpetuate it. But as an aspect of Northern humour it exists, whether I like it or not. So here are some examples – make of them what you will.

To start off with the really traditional, there can't be many who don't know these two:

The Yorkshire husband to his wife: 'All the world's queer except thee and me – and even tha's a bit queer.'

A Yorkshirewoman's prayer: 'Lord, thou has tried us with many things, try us now with some brass.'

There are many stories of the Northerner looking at life solely from his point of view. For example:

A mother home from visiting her son at a military camp: 'Eh, it wer grand seein' 'Erbert marching wi' 'is platoon. An' wad you believe it, they was *all* out of step except our lad!'

Then there was the schoolboy who announced at dinner: 'Ah deean't reckon mich ti oor teacher, Mum. Ah cud nobbut dua *yan* o' ten sums i' school ti day.'

An old Dalesman from Hawes was visiting London for the first time. While watching the traffic whirling round Trafalgar Square, he nodded to a policeman. 'Busy, isn't it?' said the policeman. 'Aye, and so it owt ti be,' answered the Dalesman, 'there's a trip in fra' 'Awes.'

In a discussion about monetary matters, one Yorkshireman asked his friend, 'What are you going to do about decimalization?' The friend replied, 'Nowt, I'm going to Barnsley tomorrow.'

Then there's the story quoted in *The Thoughts of Trueman Now*:

The late John Nash, who was secretary of the Yorkshire County Cricket Club for forty years, told of a match, Yorkshire *v.* Glamorgan at Harrogate on a Wednesday, Thursday and Friday, when an old-age pensioner came into his office to pay his yearly subs. Mr Nash said, 'Good morning, nice morning.' The old-age pensioner replied, 'Yes, it is a beautiful day.' Mr Nash said, 'Isn't it a pity that there are not more people in the ground here at Harrogate on such a beautiful day to see county cricket being played?' The old-age pensioner said, 'Well, I wouldn't worry too much about that Mr Nash, I think it will fill up this afternoon.' 'Why do you think that?' 'Because it's half-day at Pateley Bridge.' (Pateley Bridge being, of course, a small village 11 miles from Harrogate with a population of something that might be reaching 1,000!

Northerners also have a reputation for being unimpressed by

sheer magnitude. Here's another story from *The Thoughts of Trueman Now* about an early English cricket side touring America:

The England side visited Niagara Falls. The guide there was delighted to be telling English people all about America. He said, 'Just look at that – Niagara Falls, one of the wonders of the world. Do you realize that there are something like 60,000 gallons of water per second pouring over the top?' Billy Bates, a Yorkshireman, said, 'So there should be, there's nowt to stop it.'

And here are two often-quoted stories of Northern textile kings:

A Bradford textile manufacturer visited Chartres Cathedral. As he stood staring up at the great nave, another visitor beside him remarked, 'Magnificent, isn't it?' 'Aye,' he breathed, 'I could get a thousand looms in here.'

A couple of Heavy Woollen District manufacturers were gazing spellbound at a deep valley in Switzerland. 'Charley,' said one, 'doesn't tha think that's marvellous?' 'Aye,' said Charley, 'It 'ud mak' a champion tip.'

The 'Charley' of the above story was very likely Charles Robinson, who founded a big Batley mill at the turn of the century. He died in 1929, and many stories about him are still current, like the one he used to tell about the workman he had sacked who, after several weeks of fruitless search for another job, came to plead with Charley for his job back. 'I've been through hell since I left here, Mr Robinson, sheer hell.' Charley was unimpressed. 'Oh, aye. And did tha see any manufacturers i' hell, then?' 'No, Mr Robinson, I can't say I did, but I did see a sack with thi name on it.' 'Tak thi coit off and get back to work, lad,' said Charley. 'Tha's got a sense of humour if nowt else.'

There are many, many stories based on the premise that the simple Northern rustic has more than enough wit to triumph over townspeople, Southerners and Londoners. For example:

The hiker from the city asked the oldest inhabitant of a Dales village for a weather forecast. The old man screwed his eyes up to look at the sky. He tested the wind, and watched how the branches of the trees stirred. He looked down at his feet, thought long and then produced his opinion: 'It could do owt.'

There was a plummy-voiced Londoner dressed to the nines who said to an ancient Dales villager: 'I say, you jolly well ought to come up to town and see the sights.' 'Na, Ah just waits for t'sights to cum an' see me.'

A stranger – he may be driving a car, riding a bike or a horse, or walking, for this story is known in many country villages – asks a lad the way to Hawes, Kirkby Moorside, Pateley Bridge or somewhere. 'Ah deean't knaw,' mumbles the lad, who looks like the village idiot. 'Well, about how far is it?' 'Ah deean't knaw.' 'Is there anything you know?' 'Aye,' the lad replies, grinning broadly, 'Ah know Ah isn't *lost!*'

A Londoner, lost in the Dales: 'Say, John, my fine fellow, am I right for Pudsey?' Resenting the stranger's patronizing air, the slow Yorkshireman replies, 'Hoo did tha knaw ma name wor John?' 'Oh, I guessed it.' 'But hoo did tha knaw Ah wor a fine fellow?' 'Oh, I guessed that too.' 'Then, tha' mun guess t'way t'Pudsey.'

Ask a silly question . . . Some holidaymakers were visiting Dent in Yorkshire, and thought they could do a bit of leg-pulling with the old man working in the road. They asked him why Dent railway station was built so far from the village. ''Appen they wanted it near t'railway?'

Then there was the motorist trapped in a very narrow country lane behind a hay wagon moving at less than 4 miles an hour. The motorist soon lost patience and pushed his horn several times. The wagon stopped altogether. Eventually the wagon driver walked back, leaned against the car and asked: 'Wot's thi hurry? Ah'm movin' as fas as thoo, isn't Ah?'

The last two stories, which come from *Yorkshire Wit and Humour* by H.L. Gee, have a genuine Yorkshire flavour to them, for Leslie Gee spent years gathering stories from Yorkshire people in all walks of life. He is probably better known, both in Britain and abroad, as Francis Gay, compiler of the popular annual *Friendship Book of Francis Gay*, which was based on a feature column he wrote for the *Sunday Post* newspaper for many years. A schoolmaster by profession, as well as a writer, journalist and public speaker, Leslie Gee also became in the 1930s a researcher for the well-known *King's England* series of guidebooks which at that time were edited by Arthur Mee, of *Children's Encyclopedia* fame. In his capacity as researcher, Gee visited every village, town and city in Yorkshire, talking to everyone he met. A man of warm wit and humour himself, he could cajole people to respond with stories from their own family background and traditions, which his phenomenal memory, unaided by such modern contraptions as a tape-recorder, could recall without difficulty years later. Hence his book which, along with publications like the 'Northerner 11' column in the *Yorkshire Post*, is among the most genuine respositories of Yorkshire rustic humour.

Here are several more examples from Leslie Gee's rich collection, spotlighting the Yorkshireman's – and Yorkshire-woman's – attitude to life, romance and death.

First, an example of the business acumen of Yorkshire children. Two Leeds businessmen once took advantage of the lunch hour to visit Headingley to watch a particularly interesting match. 'Here, sonny,' called one, seeing a small boy near the gate, 'take this shilling and bring three fourpenny pies from the corner shop. If you're quick you can have a pie for yourself.' In less than no time the boy returned, breathless but triumphant. 'Eightpence change,' he gasped. 'They nobbut had *my* pie left.'

The next tale is one of the oldest of Yorkshire's stories. There was a farm labourer, only elevenpence three-farthings to the shilling. According to an East Riding version, the fellow was seen early one morning by a farmer, who exclaimed, 'Ah nivver expected meeting *thoo* so far from 'ome.' The labourer said, 'Ah've left mi job.' 'Left the farm six months afore Martinmas?' 'It were this way, maister. A while sin an owd cow died, and for weeks we'd nowt to eat on t'form but beef. Then an owd sheep died, and we'd nowt but mutton. *Noo, t'owd woman's died* – so ah've left!'

And now two stories which indicate an honest, down-to-earth view of matrimony.

A sixty-year-old bachelor mill worker suddenly got married. His bachelor friend said, 'Ah thowt thee an' me'd stay single till t'end of chapter, Sam.' 'An' Ah thowt, soa, too,' replied his friend, 'but Ah've a tender heart. Tha knows Ah'm at t'mill ivvery day, an' there's noabody at 'ome now mi sister's dead, so Ah *had* to find a wife. Shoo'll be a nice bit of company for t'dog.'

A Sheffield mechanic was nursed through a long illness by his patient and devoted wife. 'Eh, luv, you've bin wonderful good to me all these weeks. Whativver made you do it?' 'John, John,' replied the honest woman, 'who'd want a widder an' five bairns?'

And here are three no-nonsense views of dying and death.

Mary Lissie Warcup, who was over a hundred, had been at death's door for several days, then she rallied somewhat, lifted her head from the pillow, sniffed, and said to her daughter, 'Yon bit of 'am smells grandly, Maggie. Ah could just do wi' a bite.' Maggie's patience had about run out. 'Thee get on wi' thi dying,' she snapped. 'Yon's for t'funeral tea.'

William, an elderly Dalesman, made a point of attending local funerals. One year he went to no less than four, all of the wives of farmer friends. When a fifth suffered bereavement, William was troubled. His wife noticed. 'You'll be going to Mabel's funeral tomorrow?' 'Nay . . . Ah reckon Ah'll have to stay at 'ome, lass. Tha sees, any decent chap feels a bit diffident aboot keeping on accepting other folks' 'ospitality when he nivver 'as owt o't'soart of his own ti offer.'

Around Methley, they tell a tale of a mill-hand who was about to travel beyond the sound of clogs. While on his death-bed he was visited by the widow of his old friend, Bob. 'Eh, lad,' sighed the widow. 'When tha gets ti' heaven, tell ma man Ah'm all reet.' 'Well, by gum, what cheek,' the dying man replied. 'Dost think Ah'll have nowt to do all day but go clomping ower 'eaven looking for thi Bob?'

Death, of course, is always good for a joke from a professional comedian. This one, which has everything needed for a vintage joke – wife, dog and funeral – has been used in many a club. A fellow was walking down the road and he saw a hearse, and a fellow with an alsatian on a lead. Behind the fellow with the alsatian was a whole file of fellows, all walking very slowly, winding all the way down the road. And the first fellow asks, 'What is going on there? I've never seen that before at a funeral.' And one of the fellows in the file said, 'It's his wife in the hearse. She was nagging him and the alsatian flew at her and bit her head off.' 'Oh,' said the first fellow, 'I'm having some of that.' And he caught up with the fellow with the dog and said, 'Can I borrow your dog?' and the fellow with the dog said, 'Get in the back of the queue.'

But on to more cheerful matters. Here's a current joke about holidays. In a seaside shelter, two old West-Riding women were discussing holidays. 'It's all right comin' on yer holida',' said one, 'but when yer gets 'ome yer dishcloth's as stiff as buckram.'

For some reason, Bradford comes in for a knocking in current Yorkshire jokes. Here are two quoted by 'Northerner II' in the *Yorkshire Post*, which shows that even archbishops are not above telling them. Dr Coggan (formerly Archbishop of York and then Canterbury) tells of a Leeds man who was explaining the layout of the city to a visiting Bradfordian. 'There's Kirkgate, you see. That leads to the church. And yonder's Briggate. That leads to Leeds Bridge. And there's Swinegate. That leads to Bradford.'

Then there is the one about the Haworth resident, fed up with people knocking at his door to ask whether this was the house where the Brontë sisters were born, who put up a notice saying: 'The Brontë sisters were *not* born here.' This did not end his troubles. Now he gets people from Bradford knocking at the door and asking: 'Who are the Brontë sisters?'

But Yorkshiremen can combine against the common foe – a Lancastrian. At a meeting of the Yorkshire branch of the Institute of Electrical Engineers at Bradford, the guest speaker was from Manchester. 'I don't know why the Yorkshire electrical engineers should ask me to speak,' he said, 'because I'm a Lancastrian born and bred and always will be.' Came a voice from the audience: 'Have you no ambition?'

The New Sophisticates

Stemming from the 'never had it so good' relative prosperity of the late fifties and early sixties, a new taste, an appetite for the good life spread through the North and its people. Holidays abroad became commonplace, and vast new Las Vegas-style night clubs sprang up in such unlikely places as Batley and Wythensham. Working folk suddenly had a bit of money to spend, began to run cars, eat out, and look beyond a pint and a milk stout to give them a weekend lift.

But what was wonderful about this new sophistication was that it owed nothing to anything outside the North itself. The Northerners created their own prosperous culture – one of blue comedians, chicken-in-the-basket, lacquered wigs, plastic bouquets and glitter *lamé* dinner jackets. They went on holidays to the Balearic Islands specially tailored for their needs, stepping off their chartered 'sing-song, pass-the-hat-round-for-the-driver' jets into a quick sunburnt two weeks complete with draught ale and Cuba Libres. And when they got home they wanted more. Electric organs played 'Viva España' at Tracey's twenty-first and everything was loud and vulgar, and to hell with what they thought down South. It was as if the working people of the North suddenly found a new confidence in their own tastes and needs.

I remember staying in a little old smugglers' inn on the North-East Coast which could so easily have been chichi pseudo Cornwall. Instead the landlady led knees-ups into the early hours and made a speciality of crocheting 'cock cosies' for male guests she took a fancy to. In all colours they were – hanging round the bar. One selected one's size – complete with little pockets for testicles. Great! Great! Great! Chaucer would have loved it.

Things have calmed down a bit up North now. Harry Ramsden's Chip Shop still has chandeliers, though the Batley Variety Club's gone, but folk still go out to eat in the kind of places which are designed for them and them alone, absolutely uncompromisingly so – like Gloria Anderson's 'olde world' inn, described here in a gastronomic report by Gordon Burn which first appeared in the *Sunday Times*.

Where the Elite Meet to Eat

© *(The Sunday Times)*

Gloria Anderson has built her reputation on the big production number: when you eat at Ye Olde World Earl Grey Inn, the restaurant she runs with her husband, Tot, the blue jokes, belly laughs and digs in the ribs all come *tout compris*.

'Where the Elite Meet to Eat' boasts the menu, available now as a paperback. And it's true; on occasion they do. When they can find it.

West Kyo is very nearly at the geographical centre of an area the planners have marked down as 'Category D' – as in Dead or Dying. Which, these days, is what most of the villages around Stanley in County Durham officially are.

There used to be a time when every man who thought of the Earl Grey as his local earned his living down the mine, but now there isn't a working pit – and very few working miners – anywhere near.

Most of the colliery terraces have been demolished or have fallen into disrepair, although the occasional louvred shutter and dimpled bow window indicate that strangers from as far afield as Sunderland and Newcastle have recently swelled the population of West Kyo to about 150.

It was a sign of the times that the back room at the Earl Grey – 'Howick Lodge' nowadays – was a discotheque of sorts by the time Tot and Gloria Anderson took the place over. But she soon put a stop to all that. Within months it was Tudor-look beams and Vince Hill tapes and chicken-in-the-basket. 'Local Trade' was not encouraged and it still isn't. Anybody not coming up to Mrs A.'s very high standards very quickly gets the elbow. There is a 'dress requirement' and she doesn't expect to have to spell it out.

'They just *come* dressed,' she says. '*They* know. Anybody I don't fancy, I say, "Have you a table booked?" There's no public bar now, you see. The only locals we get are local *business*

137

people. You can't have workclothes on a seat where a lady might be going to sit in a white dress.'

And although Gloria Anderson might appear at lunchtime in jumbo rollers done up in a wet-look scarf, at dinnertime she sets out to stun; eye-lashes like garden rakes, fingernails like pearlized pink tusks.

The Andersons' idea at the beginning had been to get in, make a modest profit on their very modest investment, and get out again while the going was good. But the barsnacks were elaborated on to meet a growing demand. Before they knew it they were a pub no longer but a restaurant serving up everything from tripe and onions, frog-leg fritters and noodles and wild boar fillets with *foie gras*, to chicken on an oak leaf and steak on a plank – all this in a dying pit village on the way to nowhere.

The public bar became 'The Nook and Cranny', and 'Howick Lodge' in the back was embellished with 'Dickensian' windows and a chicken-spit, and Tot Anderson's own distinctive contribution, a heavy wooden cart wheel that is fixed to the ceiling and revolves on its axle to dispense the ingredients of the Large Popular Cocktails that are one of the Earl Grey's many novel features.

Normal helpings are so generous that spaghetti bolognaise, moussaka and beefburgers Viennese all figure on the Weight Watchers' Menu, along with marzipan-stuffed peach and fruit tart with spoil-yourself cream. And there's no holding back on the trimmings which, in fact, have become Mrs A.'s *forte*: nothing is served up that doesn't have a frilly collar, rosettes of piped potato, and a chrysanthemum and a paper parasol stuck in it. Her floral displays, using herbed tripe as a base, have been known to take the breath away. 'All my food looks as though it was *designed*,' she admits, 'rather than cooked in an oven. You've got to be artistic with food, I always think. My staff have it drilled into them that people eat with their eyes. "Is your chef Continental?" one of the waitresses was asked. "No,' she said, "she's Mrs Kirk. She lives up the bank."'

And her inventiveness knows no bounds. The seafood salad, all fresh but with a tinful of sardines on top for good measure, comes in an authentic-looking shell which she found, however, in the bathroom department at Fenwicks. It's intended for use as a soap dish.

The Earl Grey made *The Good Food Guide* in 1976 and the *Egon Ronay Guide* in 1977. It has appeared in neither guide since, which has caused Mrs Anderson no grief.

'When you're in these blasted things,' she says, 'you stand to be shot at by every nut and crank who wants to complain. We do very nicely thank you without it. Look.' The visitors' book is always to hand, but she no longer needs to consult its pages.

'Lady Beaverbrook's butler I've had. Paddy McNee from Metro Radio . . . people from Japan, look . . . I've had a Chelsea pensioner in, David Bellamy, although I don't think he signed the book. I had a girl in from Girton College, Cambridge. And a whole lot of editors one day who had the gourmet meal then tape-recorded their comments. Lawrie McMenemy's been, but I don't think he signed the book either. I once had an OBE come from Kelso. Fancy – Kelso. I don't think he signed the book, but he was an OBE.'

Nothing, though, prepared her for the visit in March last year that threw the whole of West Kyo into confusion and had the *Stanley News* man leaping for his bike. Elton John and his entourage arrived about six on the Wednesday and put away several game pies; returned the following night for more game pies and then, on the Friday, dispatched a flunkey with an order for yet more pies to take back to London.

'Hope you enjoyed the Screw,' Mrs Anderson wrote familiarly in the note she attached, adding that it was a pity he'd left the fruity bits. This was a reference of course to the largest and most popular of her Large Popular Cocktails, and Elton's favourite, the Slow Easy Comfortable Screw Against the Wall. To a mixture of Sloe gin, Southern Comfort, vodka, orange juice, the liquorice liqueur Galliano and ice, add one banana, half-peeled, with the peeled end dipped in chocolate and the base garlanded in borage flowers; clementines decorated with bits of black grape; green grapes; apple; strawberry; a sliver each of orange, grapefruit, lemon and cucumber; the whole to be decorated with Japanese umbrellas, rose cocktail sticks and seasonal flowers. And not just for Elton John either, but for everybody. 'That,' Mrs Anderson says, 'is normal. It's a lovely effect.'

When they started, Gloria, who hadn't had a cooking lesson in her life, would sit and wait for inspiration, and Tot would get it all down in writing. She did all the cooking herself in those days, but she employs a staff of twenty part-timers now. The vine leaves, which she grows next door in the bathroom, are still her province; and she always does what the menu now describes as the Elton John pie.

To show how far sophisticated entertaining has had to come to reach Gloria Anderson's heights, here is a story from the 1950s. It is told by Derrick Boothroyd, writer, novelist and once a Batley newspaper reporter. In *There's Nowt So Queer as Folk* he describes the social highlight of Batley's year, the annual mayor's ball:

> A unique feature of the supper arrangement in the council chamber – where the more important guests ate – was the serving of tea. John Gregson, the film actor, was invited to the Mayor's Ball when he was in Batley for the filming of *Value for Money* (based on the book by Derrick Boothroyd). There were wine glasses on the table and when the waitress came round with a bottle of Graves and poured him out a quarter of a glass, he presumed it was for tasting and quaffed the lot. The waitress regarded him in horror. 'That was to drink t'toasts wi'. There's tea coming if you're that thirsty.'

Somehow she seems to make more sense than Gloria.

Conclusion

So that, my friend, is Northern humour. When you consider our history I doubt if the North could have survived without it. Still, life's funny that way. If privilege and good living produced laughter, we'd have rocked at gags from Guildford or Bagshot, or listed the side-splitting comics from Bucks and Berks instead of Bolton and Bradford.

I'm proud to be Northern, proud of the North. At the risk of losing friends and influencing people the wrong way, I do my bit to keep its humorous flag flying in my little patch of SW13. People often say to me, 'If you love the North and its people so much, why don't you live there?' I think it would be extremely selfish if all Northerners restricted themselves to the North. It would be as if all Christians had stayed in Palestine. It's the duty of every Northerner to carry his philosophy of life and humour to every corner of the earth.

To wind up, here are two excerpts from Granada's 'The Comedians', the first one in the style of the maestro Jimmy James:

When you come in late and you don't want to wake her up and you are tracking across the bedroom floor walking on cornflakes. She's asleep with one eye open – strange how you girls become Shakespearean actresses at four o'clock in the morning.

'Cum 'ere.' 'I've only been with the lads.' 'Cum 'ere.' 'Don't be like that . . .' 'Get your hands off me, don't you touch me. Go back where you bin! Who do you think you are coming home to me and the children at this hour of the morning?' I said there was nowhere else open. 'Staggering round this bedroom half drunk!' I said I had run out of money otherwise I'd have been . . . 'Say daft things when you're drunk, don't you?' 'Is me dinner 'ot?' She said it should be, it's bin on the back of the fire since 6 o'clock.

My wife, now, there's a woman . . . I think. Eighteen stone, she is, she's like a yeti in knickers. No matter where she sits, she's next to you. I have to kneel on my bed to see if it's daylight. And she's thick – she set the alarm for six and there's only three of us. She went to the butcher's and said she wanted a chicken. He said, 'Do you want a pullet?' and she said, 'No, Ah brought me shopping trolley.'

'I'll never forget the honeymoon. You know, after the ham-salad reception me dad cum up. 'Y'know, son' – he's known me since I was that big, me dad – he said, 'Well, son, you're married; are you going to be a man tonight? Or a mouse tomorrow night?' I said, 'A rat – last night.'

I've recently been researching a film script in Pennsylvania. Let me quote you a piece written about my visit in the local rag: 'Friends of his describe Welland's humour as being "insulting like Dan Rickles, only drier". It took a while to get used to, but after you are around him for a while you realize it's warm and not overheavy. You begin to give as good as you get and it works.' Amen to that!

So if you are a Northerner, wherever you go keep the old flag flying, carry the battle to the enemy; be natural – naturally funny. If you are not from the North, let your hair down; have a go!

NON-FICTION

GENERAL
☐ The Chinese Mafia   Fenton Bresler   £1.50
☐ The Piracy Business   Barbara Conway   £1.50
☐ Strange Deaths   John Dunning   £1.35
☐ Shocktrauma   John Franklin & Alan Doelp   £1.50
☐ The War Machine   James Avery Joyce   £1.50

BIOGRAPHY/AUTOBIOGRAPHY
☐ All You Needed Was Love   John Blake   £1.50
☐ Clues to the Unknown   Robert Cracknell   £1.50
☐ William Wordsworth   Hunter Davies   £1.95
☐ The Family Story   Lord Denning   £1.95
☐ The Borgias   Harry Edgington   £1.50
☐ Rachman   Shirley Green   £1.50
☐ Nancy Astor   John Grigg   £2.95
☐ Monty:The Making of a General 1887-1942   Nigel Hamilton   £4.95
☐ The Windsors in Exile   Michael Pye   £1.50
☐ 50 Years with Mountbatten   Charles Smith   £1.25
☐ Maria Callas   Arianna Stassinopoulos   £1.75
☐ Swanson on Swanson   Gloria Swanson   £2.50

HEALTH/SELF-HELP
☐ The Hamlyn Family First Aid Book   Dr Robert Andrew   £1.50
☐ Girl!   Brandenburger & Curry   £1.25
☐ The Good Health Guide for Women   Cooke & Dworkin   £2.95
☐ The Babysitter Book   Curry & Cunningham   £1.25
☐ Living Together   Dyer & Berlins   £1.50
☑ The Pick of Woman's Own Diets   Jo Foley   95p
☐ Coping With Redundancy   Fred Kemp   £1.50
☐ Cystitis: A Complete Self-help Guide   Angela Kilmartin   £1.00
☐ Fit for Life   Donald Norfolk   £1.35
☐ The Stress Factor   Donald Norfolk   £1.25
☐ Fat is a Feminist Issue   Susie Orbach   £1.25
☐ Fat is a Feminist Issue II   Susie Orbach   £3.50
☐ Living With Your New Baby   Rakowitz & Rubin   £1.50
☐ Related to Sex   Claire Rayner   £1.50
☐ Natural Sex   Mary Shivanandan   £1.25
☐ Woman's Own Birth Control   Dr Michael Smith   £1.25
☐ Overcoming Depression   Dr Andrew Stanway   £1.50
☐ Health Shock   Martin Weitz   £1.75

POCKET HEALTH GUIDES
☐ Depression and Anxiety   Dr Arthur Graham   85p
☐ Diabetes   Dr Alex D. G. Gunn   85p
☐ Heart Trouble   Dr Simon Joseph   85p
☐ High Blood Pressure   Dr James Knapton   85p
☐ The Menopause   Studd & Thom   85p
☐ Children's Illnesses   Dr Luke Zander   85p

TRAVEL
☐ The Complete Traveller   Joan Bakewell   £1.95
☐ Time Out London Shopping Guide   Lindsey Bareham   £1.50
☐ A Walk Around the Lakes   Hunter Davies   £1.75
☐ Britain By Train   Patrick Goldring   £1.75
☐ England By Bus   Elizabeth Gundrey   £1.25
☐ Staying Off the Beaten Track   Elizabeth Gundrey   £2.95
☐ Britain at Your Feet   Wickers & Pedersen   £1.75

HUMOUR
☐ Don't Quote Me   Atyeo & Green   £1.00
☐ Ireland Strikes Back!   Seamus B. Gorrah   85p
☐ Pun Fun   Paul Jennings   95p
☐ 1001 Logical Laws   John Peers   95p
☐ The Devil's Bedside Book   Leonard Rossiter   85p

REFERENCE

☐ The Sunday Times Guide to Movies on Television	Angela & Elkan Allan	£1.50
☐ The Cheiro Book of Fate and Fortune		£1.50
☐ Hunter Davies's Book of British Lists		£1.25
☐ NME Guide to Rock Cinema	Fred Dellar	£1.50
☐ What's Wrong With Your Pet?	Hugo Kerr	95p
☐ The Drinker's Companion	Derek Nimmo	£1.25
☐ The Complete Book of Cleaning	Barty Phillips	£1.50
☐ The Oscar Movies from A-Z	Roy Pickard	£1.25
☐ Collecting For Profit	Sam Richards	£1.25
☐ Islam	D. S. Roberts	£1.50
☐ Questions of Motoring Law	John Spencer	£1.25
☐ Questions of Law	Bill Thomas	£1.25

GAMES AND PASTIMES

☐ The Hamlyn Book of Wordways 1		75p
☐ The Hamlyn Family Quiz Book		85p

WAR

☐ The Battle of Malta	Joseph Attard	£1.50
☐ World War 3	Edited by Shelford Bidwell	£1.50
☐ The Black Angels	Rupert Butler	£1.35
☐ Gestapo	Rupert Butler	£1.50
☐ Hand of Steel	Rupert Butler	£1.35
☐ The Flight of the Mew Gull	Alex Henshaw	£1.75
☐ Sigh for a Merlin	Alex Henshaw	£1.50
☐ Hitler's Secret Life	Glenn B. Infield	£1.25

GARDENING

☐ 'Jock' Davidson's House Plant Book		£1.50
☐ A Vegetable Plot for Two — or More	D. B. Clay Jones	£1.00
☐ Salads the Year Round	Joy Larkcom	£1.50
☐ Gardening Tips of A Lifetime	Fred Loads	£1.50
☐ Sunday Telegraph Patio Gardening	Robert Pearson	£1.00
☐ Greenhouse Gardening	Sue Phillips	£1.25

COOKERY

☐ A-Z of Health Foods	Carol Bowen	£1.50
☐ The Giant Sandwich Book	Carol Bowen	£1.50
☐ Vegetarian Cookbook	Dave Dutton	£1.50
☐ Jewish Cookbook	Florence Greenberg	£1.50
☐ Know Your Onions	Kate Hastrop	95p
☐ Indian Cooking	Attia Hosain and Sita Pasricha	£1.50
☐ Home Preserving and Bottling	Gladys Mann	80p
☐ Home Baked Breads & Cakes	Mary Norwak	75p
